ENGLISH INSIDE AND OUT

Since 1944, the English Institute has presented work by distinguished scholars in English and American literatures, foreign literatures, and related fields. A volume of papers selected from the meeting is published annually.

Also available in the series from Routledge:

COMPARATIVE AMERICAN IDENTITIES

Race, Sex, and Nationality in the Modern Text

EDITED BY HORTENSE J. SPILLERS

English Inside and Out

THE PLACES OF LITERARY CRITICISM

EDITED WITH AN INTRODUCTION BY
SUSAN GUBAR AND JONATHAN KAMHOLTZ

**ESSAYS FROM THE 50TH ANNIVERSARY
OF THE ENGLISH INSTITUTE**

ROUTLEDGE   NEW YORK AND LONDON

Published in 1993 by

Routledge
An imprint of Routledge, Chapman and Hall, Inc.
29 West 35th Street
New York, NY 10001

Published in Great Britain by

Routledge
11 New Fetter Lane
London EC4P 4EE

Jonathan Goldberg's essay is published in a different version in his book *Sodometries: Renaissance Texts, Modern Sexualities* (© 1992 Stanford University Press). The publishers gratefully acknowledge Stanford's permission to print here the version delivered at the English Institute.

Library of Congress Cataloging-in-Publication Data

English inside and out: the places of literary criticism / edited with an introduction by Susan
   Gubar and Jonathan Kamholtz.
     p. cm.
   "Papers from the 50th anniversary of the English Institute."
   Includes bibliographical references.
   ISBN 0-415-90667-9.—ISBN 0-415-90668-7
   1. English literature—History and criticism—Theory, etc.—Congresses. 2. American literature—History and criticism—Theory, etc.—Congresses. 3. American literature—Study and teaching (Higher)—Congresses. 4. English literature—Study and teaching (Higher)—Congresses. I. Gubar, Susan. II. Kamholtz, Jonathan. III. English Institute.
PR21.E53 1993
820.9—dc20
                                                 92-24503
                                                    CIP

ISBN 0-415-90667-9 (HB)
ISBN 0-415-90668-7 (PB)

Contents

Introduction

SUSAN GUBAR AND JONATHAN KAMHOLTZ

A funny thing happened on the way to the 50th anniversary meeting of the English Institute. The study of literature made headlines. *Newsweek, Time,* the *New Republic,* the *Village Voice, Harper's, Atlantic,* the *New York Times Magazine,* the *Wall Street Journal,* and the *National Review:* all these publications and many others featured articles during the last two years on the state of the humanities in general or departments of English in particular. The national news offered regular installments of what used to be merely departmental controversies. In part because of this, the supervisors of the August 1991 English Institute—an organization whose members meet yearly at Harvard University to hear and respond to scholarly papers— decided to focus three sessions on "The Institutions of English," asking participants to consider where we are going, where we have been, and indeed who "we" are.

In part: there were a number of other considerations that caused us to put together a series of papers on the sociology of knowledge in our discipline. First, because it was the 50th anniversary of the Institute, we wanted to assemble some of the critics who had made their mark on it either as speakers, organizers of sessions, or editors of volumes. They constitute a living history of much of what has been best about our profession for the past half century. In 1948, for example, when Leslie Fiedler—then of Montana State University—spoke on "Myth in the Later Plays of Shakespeare," his audience included D.A. Robertson, E. Talbot Donaldson, and W.K. Wimsatt; on the same panel, Northrop Frye introduced his essay on "The Argument of Comedy" and later that evening Wallace Stevens spoke on

"Imagination as Value." Second, we were struck with the changes in our membership and programs over the last decades. Where had all the grownups gone? What happens when the members of what Barbara Herrnstein Smith calls an "oppositional" vanguard find themselves in control of an organization? An older generation had clearly made room for a more diverse younger group of scholars—if the results of Oedipal titanism can be put so dispassionately—but we hoped our sessions would constitute a kind of family reunion. What—and who—can heal such wounds? Third, we expected that such a reunion might enable us to assess the significance of an Institute which has prided itself on presenting critical innovations and innovators as they embarked. What could be learned from a retrospective of new beginnings?

Predictably, though, our local agenda dovetailed with the concerns of participants in the audience and the speakers themselves, many of whom were acutely aware of the media blitz that had imbued the humanities with a weird, even hallucinatory, notoriety. Clearly the nature and place of literary controversy had changed vastly in a half century. Popular articles and best-selling books had appeared that were directed to—or more frequently against—contemporary trends in English departments across the country. Canon revision; emancipatory agendas of approaches grounded in class, race, gender, and sexual orientation; the political import of "third world" or "postcolonial" discourse; the "new" historicizing of literary texts; the purported ahistoricizing of deconstruction: these approaches and those who represented them had played prominent roles at the Institute and now they had come under fierce, sustained attack by journalists, educators, and administrators whose strategy frequently seemed to involve exaggerating the impact of ideas they were determined to deride.

Newsweek, for example, denounced the "new McCarthyism" of the "thought police" on campus, while the *Atlantic* featured Dinesh D'Souza's "Illiberal Education," a militant call-to-arms infused by the belief that "resistance on campus to the academic revolution is outgunned and sorely needs outside reinforcement." Evidently "the whole world is watching" was taking on a new meaning. A cover of *New York* magazine sustained this culture war mentality by featuring a photograph of Camille Paglia under the banner "Woman Warrior." While President Bush preached against the tyranny of political correctness at the University of Michigan, a column in *Time* magazine lamented that everything is "Upside Down in the Groves of Academe," where students are subjected to "a literature class that equates Shakespeare and the novelist Alice Walker not as artists but as fragments of sociology." *Time,* continuing the rhetorical strategy of denouncing the most visible representatives of the academy for being both dangerously influential with undergraduates and profoundly out of touch with American society, wrote that "obfuscatory course titles and eccentric reading lists frequently are wedded to a combative political agenda or outlandish views of the nation's culture and values."

These charges are not far removed from those promulgated recently in the books of Allan Bloom, Roger Kimball, and Charles Sykes, as well as the speeches of William Bennett and Lynne Cheney, past and present heads of the National Endowment for the Humanities. Disciples of the humanities used to pass on their ideas in an almost masonic secrecy: what else was graduate school? For a myth had been fostered ages ago in which the hushed seminar room stood at the center of an isolated, even cloistered, ivory tower, with all the erotic attraction accorded such intimacies. Now, however, paradigms are being noisily debated in sound bites at press conferences. Who would have thought so many people were watching or listening?

In the midst of the brouhaha, some public rebuttals surfaced. Barbara Ehrenreich's think-piece "Teach Diversity—With a Smile" appeared in *Time* to point out that "multiculturalism" has become a banner under which the right wing encourages the media to lump together deconstructionists and feminists, African-American and popular culture scholars, as if they were a homogeneous, dangerous party of wild-eyed, fortysomething "tenured radicals." The *Village Voice* ran a long article by Michael Bérubé on "Political Correctness and the Media's Big Lie" in which the tongue-in-cheek author admits to being "a young faculty member," to knowing another "young faculty member," and to plotting a scheme to topple the West: his friend will kneel behind the West on all fours. Then Mr. Bérubé himself will "push it backward over him." In a MacNeil/Lehrer NewsHour, Catharine Stimpson justified the Modern Language Association's resistance to NEH, specifically to Carol Ianonne's nomination to the National Council of Humanities, but Stimpson was driven to defend herself against Lynne Cheney, avowing "I'm a Rotarian's daughter from Bellingham, Washington. I believe in the Bill of Rights."

The atmosphere that instills such defensiveness even in an eloquent spokesperson like Stimpson may well seem alarming to those she represents. As Hortense Spillers, the Chair of the Supervisors of the English Institute that year, proposed in an essay in the *Women's Review of Books,* the current climate means we need to meet the "pot-shots . . . taken at 'theory,' " as well as the "disarray among the political left of center," with "critical/theoretical project[s] more grounded in public and ethical responsiveness." Spillers expressed an urgency which many of the other organizers of the English Institute shared. We decided, then, to invite speakers whose contributions to the Institute demonstrated their commitment to critical, theoretical, or pedagogic projects grounded in public and ethical responsiveness.

All but one of the essays in this book were delivered at the 1991 English Institute, chiefly at the three sessions on "The Institutions of English."

However, two notable omissions in the volume need to be acknowledged, for their absence reflects contemporary issues in the profession. First, because we sought contributors who acknowledged their civic roles, in one case precisely such responsibilities made participation impossible: Edward Said, who had been scheduled to appear, was unable to attend because his public role as spokesperson for the Palestinian cause required him to be out of the country on short notice. Second, because our speakers exhibited an exceptional commitment to social issues, in one case exactly such a commitment made inclusion of the presentation in this volume impossible: Houston A. Baker, Jr., whose talk in Cambridge provocatively speculated on the failures of the academy to meet the needs of African-Americans, fused scholarly discourse with political activism in an extraordinary enactment of critical passion. We regret that the visual and improvisatory nature of his performance could not be recaptured in print here.

Like the sessions at the English Institute, *English Inside and Out* begins with meditations that examine the transformation of English studies in a period when most teachers feel there is no single canon of great books upon which we can all agree to base a liberal and literate education. Taken together, the first three essays ask what will bind us together if we have discarded the idea of an established set of texts, a canon of literary material to be covered in the English classroom? Although Alvin Kernan, Leslie Fiedler, and Geoffrey Hartman respond quite differently to the influx of new sorts of texts and questions into the literature classroom, all three affirm the value of English studies at least in part by cherishing and sustaining a critical voice supple enough to collaborate with the past while strong enough to challenge it.

Alvin Kernan opened the sessions, as he begins this volume, by posing the central problems. What has happened to texts and the traditional questions we asked of them? What is our profession if we no longer even agree on common objects and ends of study? And, most important, what role should English departments play in a society that increasingly marginalizes print culture, placing less and less value on the book? Equally concerned with canonical changes, Leslie Fielder contemplates the institutionalization of his own dissenting voice. The revisionist canon for which he fought, he now thinks, may have all of the vices of any fixed canon with none of the pleasures of the traditional one. (These are matters germane to the English Institute itself, where the question "Where did the literature go?" has been linked to "Where did the audience go?") While Fiedler worries that the new critics of the canon will eventually encase teachers in straitjackets as stultifying as those employed by old defenders of the great books, Geoffrey Hartman meditates on the ways in which the interpretive skills taught by professors of English schooled in the poetry, drama, and philosophy of the past can negotiate among the various kinds of texts—

films, ads, TV shows, popular novels—that currently find their way into our classrooms.

Hartman's speculations on the nature of the basic unit of critical exchange within the profession, the critical essay, function to contextualize the meditations of Henry Louis Gates, Jr., and Jane Gallop, both of whom seek to use scholarly disputes within African-American and women's studies as a way of bringing complex social problems into public debate. Gates, who has graciously allowed us to publish his "The Welcome Table," traces the generational tensions between James Baldwin and the younger black intellectuals who demoted him from his role as spokesperson for the race, a status he himself disavowed. Gates recalls how he, as a twenty-two-year-old journalist, met with Baldwin in Provence and then moves backward to describe how, as a fourteen-year old, he encountered Baldwin's essays. Through this autobiographical retrospective, Gates provides a portrait of his evolution as an African-American scholar, a genealogy of his own efforts to use African-American studies to examine what Baldwin also articulated, namely the equivocal sympathies and clashing allegiances of any critic who seeks to enact his criticism in the world.

Also attentive to the critic's social responsibility, Jane Gallop describes the most recent stage of feminist criticism as an attempt to account for ethnic issues as gender studies become increasingly institutionalized. According to Gallop, the dramatic evolution of African-American and women's studies over the past few decades—the increasing visibility of these disciplines within English departments—need not constitute co-optation. Instead, it can allow both fields to jettison simplistic universalizing about race and gender, to generate sophisticated paradigms for comprehending differences among and within such monolithic categories as "women" or "blacks" or "Native Americans." Just as Gates and Gallop examine the relationship of African-American and women's studies scholarship to contemporary communities of readers and writers, the last five essays in this volume continue to shift the focus from inside to outside the academy, challenging the distinctions between the scholarly work of English studies and the ethical, political, and pedagogic responsibilities of its practitioners.

Exemplifying the impact of cultural studies, Jonathan Goldberg and John Brenkman use new texts—Goldberg's ad and his account of laws against homosexuality, Brenkman's discussion of political definitions of citizenship—to tackle social issues of inclusion and exclusion, scapegoating and partisanship, that affect our students, ourselves, and our tasks in and out of the university. Focusing on the profession of English within the university as an economic reality that exists in the "outside" social realm, Stanley Fish challenges the notion of the academy as an isolated, cloistered retreat. Fish contrasts our appetite for performance and professional success, on the one hand, with our reluctance to enjoy the show, on the other. The inhibitions of academics have not helped us respond to the recent attacks on the ways the humanities are professed. Though we seem to have felt ourselves effective enough to have undertaken curricular reform in the first place, we appear to believe that we are professionally powerless.

Fish's humorous analysis of the masochistic self-image of English professors and his insistence that this self-image damages our commerce with the world as well as our effectiveness within the university imply that literary critics need to stop insulating the world inside the academy from the political and economic marketplace around it, a point evident also in the two essays that conclude this volume. In quite different ways, both Gerald Graff and Eve Kosofsky Sedgwick call on practitioners of literary criticism to merge pedagogy, political activism, and a kind of public performance. Graff argues that the national debate waits to be joined by those who can learn to write about the humanities in a form that can be understood by the public, even if we must counter sound bite with sound bite. Like Fish, Graff wonders why we cling to our political superiority or our theoretical purity, if it means we are only conversing with ourselves and thereby unable to defend our critical endeavors. The urgency of the issues that constitute our national, political texts makes Sedgwick take critical questions out to the picket line. We conclude with her account of critical inquiry inside and outside the gay studies classroom because she raises questions beyond simple resolution about the degrees of control one ever has over one's most dedicated performance.

Indeed, performance—as it was enacted in Cambridge at the English Institute in August of 1991 and as it becomes thematized in the last essays of this book—emerges as a crucial trope in thinking about the critic's role in the classroom, at the conference, in the department meeting, at public forums, in political arenas. Many of the essays in this collection envision critical interpretation or intervention, as it is often called, as a form of performance. Sometimes it seems as though criticism has become a road show, complete with its own traveling superstars. In part, the profession we toil in now has become brash (and the record will show that the English Institute has been at times one of the brasher parts of it). But it is more complicated than supposing that we used to perform inside the academy and now we need to follow out the implications of our act and dramatize ourselves outside as well. What kind of self is the performing self?

Those who profess literature seem once again ready to reintroduce the personal and the private to their public voice, merging the grandiose and the intimate, the scholarly and the sincere. Such gestures link Stephen Greenblatt, looking at the seats next to his own on an airplane at the close of *Renaissance Self-Fashioning,* with Nancy Miller's new book on autobiographical criticism, *Getting Personal,* and with Eve Kosofsky Sedgwick's moving vision of herself, prostrate on television, in her essay in this volume.

Will a shift toward performance reinvigorate the notion of critic as activist which was part of the heritage Leslie Fiedler brought to the sessions from the start? Or is it a sign of the times, a desperate reaction against the marginalization of the humanities in our society or a defiant protest against the desolation facing educators in a time of falling budgets and rising social ills?

Despite the pessimism our contributors express about the state of American society and its centers of higher education, the energy and verve of their productions testify to a renewed engagement with English Studies that makes less surprising the plethora of phrases they and other colleagues suggested as titles for this anniversary volume, all of which illuminate our project here. In the spirit of our speakers, who wrote in a refreshingly comprehensible manner, we tried to find a title that included no arcane or fractured words. Some suggestions we rejected included *English Now* and *The Current Culture of English Studies,* though these emphasized the topicality of the subject and positioned us in relation to the network of controversies the English Institute has foregrounded. *The Functions of English at the Present Time,* with its echo of Arnold, reminded us that we confront new critical tasks when many competing methodologies have undermined the closed canon of the "monuments of unageing intellect" that no longer serves all of us as touchstones. *What Was Literary Criticism?,* with its allusion to Fiedler's *What Was Literature?,* and *English After All* seemed wistful and apocalyptic, shaped by our fear that criticism may no longer have a secure place in the classroom, the conference center, or the culture. What if it is just a "virtual reality," kept alive by its enemies? *Saving English: For What?* seemed a little too messianic, *The Bondage and Discipline of English* a bit too slick and titillating.

And so we have chosen *English Inside and Out: The Places of Literary Criticism* because it captures our sense that the current debates are in part the result of blurring the boundaries between inside (the classroom, the department, the academy, the field of specialization, the Institute) and out (our various constituencies or communities). We wanted to recognize that criticism has found antagonists to whom teachers and scholars must respond. We wanted to avoid the image that the profession has turned the wagons in a circle. Also, we wanted to pay tribute to a person who was crucial in turning the English Institute inside-out, opening up its doors to new and innovative thinkers. The 50th anniversary marked the last year Marjorie Garber served as its Executive Secretary, giving a local habitation and name to the Institute the other fifty-one weeks of the year. She functioned as the spirit of the place in Cambridge, providing a procession of members old and new with welcome, a series of panel chairs with unlisted phone numbers, and several generations of programs with quiet leadership, seeing to it that our inquiries were worthy of the Institute. The editors join the members in thanking her.

There are other thanks that are due as well. Jonathan Kamholtz would like to thank Eve Sedgwick, Joshua Wilner, and Tim Gould for almost half a lifetime of good suggestions, including attending the English Institute; David Riggs for teaching him half of what he knows; and Sally Kamholtz for being his best colleague about the important things. As always, Susan Gubar is indebted to the brilliant insights of Sandra M. Gilbert; she is also grateful for the intellectual generosity and companionship of Donald Gray and Mary Jo Weaver.

In 1974, W.K. Wimsatt concluded an introduction to his anthology of Institute papers by explaining that "It is easy to contend with the fathers, to revolt against them, easy to reshape, to recolor, to contaminate received materials, easy to make our own mistakes and to reverse them, to change our minds and even to incorporate changes in our works. But not easy to execute any of these commonplaces with the kind of special reason and authority that turns them into wit and imagination." In her introduction to the papers from the 1981 meeting of the English Institute, the first time its program was devoted to issues of gender, Carolyn G. Heilbrun agreed that Wimsatt had articulated the tasks confronting feminist critics. Now, coming to terms with transformations in English Studies effected by manifold revolts and contentions, the editors of this volume are delighted by the wit and imagination evident in the reasoned authority of the meditations we have collected. Indeed, both of us share the belief that the essays gathered here (produced by "the fathers" as well as by their rebellious descendants) serve as testimony that places for literature and criticism have been found and these places are worthy of us all. The scenes of instruction have changed, as the Institute, one such scene, has changed. However, what English was and will be remains the literature we teach as well as the complex set of interpretive practices that enable us not only to understand but also to affect the aesthetic, societal, and political realms within which we abide.

1.

Plausible and Helpful Things to Say About Literature in a Time When All Print Institutions Are Breaking Down

ALVIN KERNAN

The art of letters will come to an end before A.D. 2000 . . . I shall survive as a curiosity.
—Ezra Pound[1]

The extraordinary events in the literary world over the last twenty or twenty-five years are best understood, it is my argument, as but one part of the disturbances presently occurring in all print-centered institutions such as newspapers, libraries, publishing, and education. How literature might best be preserved becomes in these circumstances an urgent question.

Since writing appeared in ancient Egypt and Mesopotamia, and especially since the print revolution began about 1450, first the manuscript and then the book have been the privileged modes of communication and information storage in Western society. "What is printed is true." Many of our major institutions have grown up around the book. Try to imagine religion, especially Judaism or Protestantism, without *The* Book, or the law without written statutes, or, to come closer to home, liberal education without the library. But now under the pressure of new electronic modes of communication book culture is so churned up that it is no exaggeration to speak of the end of the Gutenberg Age and the disintegration of its primary institutions.

Nowhere is the turmoil greater in print-based institutions than in the newspaper industry. In 1960 there were 1771 newspapers published in America; in 1990 there were 1643, and the number continues to decrease. The other day brought news of the oldest paper in Arkansas, the *Gazette,* founded in 1819, being taken over by the *Arkansas Democrat.* On December 9, 1991, the *Dallas Times Herald,* the city's oldest newspaper, ceased publication, selling its machinery to its rival, the *Morning News.* But the decrease is much greater than the raw figures show. They do not take into account the growth in the population in that thirty-year period, which could have supported additional papers, or the shift from afternoon to morning publication, with most of the afternoon papers being no longer independent but jointly operated late versions of the morning paper. In the period 1971–1977 alone the percentage of adults reading a daily paper went down from 54 to 43 per cent, and the number has continued to decrease since then. In New York in the two years after the great newspaper strike of 1963, nine dailies were reduced to three.

The newspaper world has deteriorated to the point of open violence. In London that most august of newspapers, the *Times,* was produced for years behind a barbed wire fence, with a threatening mob outside shouting threats at the workers. More recently, during 1990–1991 management and unions at the *New York Daily News* were locked in a bitter strike, each side claiming right and justice for themselves. Management, which had been losing millions a year, claimed that unless they could get rid of practices like over-manning the presses, non-competitive wages, featherbedding, inefficient work rules, ten different unions, and so on, they could not stay in business. The workers and their unions contended that management had forced them to go on strike by threatening their jobs and by running a shop in which no self-respecting journalist or pressman would want to work. Feelings ran high from the beginning, and the situation turned ugly almost at once. Newsdealers were threatened, newsstands burned, drivers assaulted, picket lines crossed, strikebreakers imported, toughs recruited to drive the delivery trucks, advertisers intimidated, papers given to the homeless to sell in the subways. There were court injunctions, picket-line scuffles, threats and cries of "scab." After the spite sale to the British media mogul, Robert Maxwell, "Maxwell's Plum," he extracted even more givebacks from the strikers than the loathed original management had asked, before stripping the paper of its assets and probably killing himself.

Newspapers offer an open and dramatic insight into how print insti-tutions are breaking down. At the point of contact in the *Daily News* strike the issues were immediate gut realities involving legal and moral rights: workers have a right to jobs and a living wage, management needs to turn a profit, freedom of the press, sanctity of contracts. But these issues, and all the fears, anger, and violence released by them, were driven ultimately by new technology that is radically changing every part of the newspaper business. One of its valedictorians speaks rightly of the newspaper as "the dove sent from the ark of mechanical society to test the waters of com-puterization."[2] Newspapers were the ultimate print product, and they cen-tered in the typesetting and printing operations. Now, the paper can not only be written but composed, produced, and even distributed in some cases from an editor's word processor. The center of operations has therefore shifted to the editorial and reporting functions, making many of the old typesetters and pressmen redundant. The morgue, circulation, advertising, classifieds can now be managed centrally; wire services, stock indexes, sports scores and other material can be sent directly to the computer and automatically set. Electronic technology has secondary as well as primary effects on newspapers. Young people grow up as TV watchers, not newspaper readers; many of the news and entertainment functions of the newspapers have shifted to TV; and most national advertising—beer, cars, detergent, toothpaste—has left the papers to go to TV, taking more than half of the newspapers' advertising income with it. All of this puts tremendous financial and organizational pressures on newspapers—money is short, the ancient practices of Chapel and Guild are challenged, savings from technology have to be realized.

In other print institutions where the disruption has been less violent and less widely reported than in the newspaper troubles, change has been no less painful and relentless. There too, though the cause-and-effect pattern is less clear, electronics are everywhere at work. Libraries, for example, particularly the great research collections like the British Library and the Library of Congress, are the monuments of the printed book, and at every level of operation they are in deep trouble. Columbia University decided in 1990 to close its prestigious library school—except, presciently, the rare-book section—on the grounds that library science no longer has a place in a research university! And in the last twelve years, fourteen other library schools, out of a total of fifty-three, have closed, including those at the University of Chicago, the University of Southern California, and Vanderbilt University.

As if to represent what is happening, large numbers of books are literally disappearing before our eyes from the shelves of the older libraries. It has long been known that the pulp paper made after about 1870 disintegrates over a period of time because the alum-rosin that helps it take ink evenly combines with moisture to form an acid that breaks down the binding between the pulp fibers. The deterioration can be halted by a difficult process of deacidification, and some of the books can be saved by being microfilmed. But these remedies are so labor-intensive and therefore expensive as to make it possible to save only a relatively few of the 40 per cent of the books in major research collections in the United States that will soon be too fragile to handle. A recent report concluded that "all book repositories are self-destructing time bombs."[3]

There seems to be no good news in the libraries these days, for they are particularly vulnerable to the economic squeeze. The number of books and journals continues to increase yearly, and their cost continues to outstrip both the general rate of inflation and the rate of growth of library resources.

Journal prices have risen by 400 per cent in the past twenty years, and books by almost 40 per cent in the past five. As a result library acquisition of books and monographs has declined by 30 per cent, at a time when the amount of published material is increasing exponentially. Despite cuts in purchases, cataloguing arrearages continue to mount, and if libraries continue to acquire new materials at the present rate, much less at the rate they might wish to, they will have to build expensive new space at a cost of tens of millions of dollars, with associated ongoing maintenance and operating expenses.

Across the country in a time of recession libraries are being closed, hours shortened, services cut, collections falling into disrepair. New York City reduced its library budget for 1992 by nearly 30 per cent. "These are the worst cutbacks that libraries have gone through in this century," says Linda F. Crismond, executive director of the American Library Association. "Even in the Depression," before the TV era, that is, "when everything was being closed, libraries were kept open." But now libraries "are planning for disaster."[4] An unpublished Mellon Foundation study of academic libraries by Anthony Cummings shows conclusively that contrary to common wisdom academic research libraries have been getting an increasingly smaller proportion of the overall academic budget in the 1970s and 1980s in comparison to the instructional and administrative portions of the budget. Library budgets have over the years gone up at about a 2.7 per cent annual rate in constant dollars, but increasingly large amounts of expenditures have gone to an ever increasing number of serials and to the purchase of electronic equipment and software. At the same time the number of monographs published has increased rapidly, as have their prices, tripling in the last fifteen years, at a time when the cost of electronics has been diminishing. As a result gross acquisitions of books have been slowing down for twenty years, and the proportion acquired of total books published has been falling off even more sharply.

Book publishing is in no better shape than the libraries that buy its product. Indeed, the two, like drowning swimmers, intensify one another's problems. The Gutenberg Age is ending, it is important to emphasize, not with a whimper but a bang, the way most things, savings banks or amusement parks, end in this country, in surfeit rather than shortage. According to the R.R. Bowker *Book Publishing Annual*, about 11,000 titles were published in the United States in 1950, when commercial television first appeared. By 1960, 15,000; by 1980 approximately 42,000; by 1989, 53,446. (Interestingly, titles in literature went down from 3,085 in 1970 to 2,298 in 1989, having dropped off sharply in the 1970s and "recovered" somewhat in the 1980s.) Income during this time rose even faster, from $500 million in 1950 to more than $7 billion in 1979. But prosperity is only on the surface, for during the same time the average sale of single titles of trade books has dropped below 2500, and the standard university press monograph now sells only about 700 copies, almost all to libraries. Both trade and university press publishers have responded to the downward curve in sales by escalating prices and doubling the titles published, which pushes sales down still further—stagflation.

Returns from bookstores have reached landslide proportions, and the publishers' best customers, the libraries, are going broke trying to buy the increasing number of books at inflationary prices. Just to add to the difficulties, the Federal Government now taxes unsold inventories of published books in a way that makes it uneconomic for commercial publishers to keep printed books in stock past the end of any tax year. Thus the perennial difficulty of getting the novels of Hardy or, as I recently found to my surprise, the poems of Philip Larkin that are needed for classes, a shortage that makes the Norton Anthology a perennial best-seller. The publication and pricing of books are technologically obsolescent. Most publishers are still refusing to work from authors' disks, on the grounds that corrections and system compatibility are problematical, preferring to pay to have the pages set. The economy of publishing belongs to another century. "If the cover price of a book is $20, then at least 40 per cent, or $8, will go to the retailer. Of the remaining $12, perhaps $3 will go to the distributors who ship the books from the printers to the bookstores. Of the remaining $9, it might cost $3 actually to produce the book. The author receives $2 and the publisher keeps $4. All these numbers vary considerably, but as a rule of thumb a book's cover price is six to eight times the production cost."[5]

In an attempt to deal with the financial squeeze, the great publishing houses associated with bibliographic high culture, Scribners and Random House, for example, are disappearing into communications conglomerates. Pantheon, an imprint associated with books of quality, was recently reorganized for having a negative bottom line. Small bookstores proliferate, but the big business is done by high-volume shopping-center chains like Waldenbooks, whose corporate attitude towards books was not long ago stated bluntly by Harry Hoffman, its CEO. Books, he said, are "ill conceived products . . . filled with too many pages and too much small print to be able to counter things like Nintendo or television."[6] In stores run on this principle books with low sales are soon eliminated, and the half-life of all books is sharply curtailed. Unsold books go quickly to that sad limbo of the book, the remainder house, or the shredding machine to save warehousing costs and taxes on inventory.

But does it make any difference in the quality of books published? Jacob Weisberg, in a recent article titled, "Rough Trade," argues that it very much does. In the search for blockbusters that will enhance the reputation of the editor in the world of big-bucks publishing, he says, traditional editing has nearly disappeared—"Who has time or interest to go line by line over long dull books any longer, when the martinis and the crisp linen of good restaurants beckon?" As a result, books are filled with misspellings and poor grammar; they are too long and poorly organized. Head-hunting editors armed with million dollar advances search for sensational plot outlines, not completed manuscripts. Recently, to offer one example, the head of the holding company that controls Simon and Schuster decided, *mirabile dictu,* that the blockbusting novel *American Psycho,* by Brent Easton Ellis, about a series of crimes in which women are dismembered with chainsaws, was so distasteful that the company would forgive its advance of several hundred thousand dollars in order to avoid publishing it. But what appalls some glints with the possibility of profit for others, and instantly that white knight of the publishing world, Sonny Mehta, the shoot-from-the-hip head of Random House, rode in to pick up the contract, talking of First Amendment rights and the sanctity of the creative imagination. It is sobering in these circumstances to recall the Random House Fall catalog for 1951, "a discriminating twenty books: fiction by William Faulkner, Truman Capote, Nancy Mitford, John O'Hara, and Par Lagerkvist, as well as the complete novels of Jane Austen, and several minor writers long forgotten."[7] Books are increasingly commodities: "The seven-figure advances for unwritten novels, the obsequious profiles in 'serious' magazines, the power of agents, the editors hopping from house to house to unemployment, the pervasive networking and shopping and thumping and scratching and oil and rising and falling."[8]

All of the institutions of the book are in trouble at the present time, but none more desperately than an educational system built around the linked Gutenberg skills of reading and writing. Once the hope of our society, we now hear horror stories of weapons in the classroom, pregnancy, drugs, venereal disease. Half of the students are said not to know which century the American Civil War was fought in or who fought it; a majority of students were not able to locate Iraq on the map at the time of the recent Gulf War.

Literacy is central to all print institutions, but it is absolutely critical in education. Reading is a difficult skill that must be learned, which TV watching and listening are not, and reading skills are dropping off so rapidly that we now matter-of-factly speak of a "literacy crisis." A survey conducted by the U.S. Census Bureau in 1982 found 13 per cent of U.S. adults to be illiterate, and the *New York Times* reported in 1988 that 10 per cent of all people of reading age, about 23 million, cannot read and write well enough to perform everyday functions. Among those who can read but choose not to, the so-called "aliterate," various surveys show that something like 60 per cent of adult Americans never read a book of any kind, and a majority of the remainder read no more than one book a year.

The ability to read will probably never disappear entirely, even if it is used only to read information off the word processor screen or CD ROMs, but as information becomes more and more available from visual images and from the voices of television and radio, reading is becoming less familiar and less intensive in all areas of life. SAT scores measuring verbal ability continue to slip relentlessly, declining from 466 to 424 between 1967 and 1990. Some of the slippage is attributable, as many in education have defensively pointed out, to the extension of college education to much wider and less well-educated groups than earlier. But a nobler cause does not make the effects any the less troubling. The public view is that the spread of illiteracy is reversible with enough effort and money, but it is likely that we have already come as close to universal literacy as we are going to get, and that as the high Gutenberg Age wanes and the TV era takes over, reading will become less common, and with it the even more difficult skill of writing. With the disappearance of these skills our primary and secondary educational system is falling apart before our eyes.

Literature's connection with print is obvious in its dependence on printed texts and on reading. I tried to show in some detail in *Samuel Johnson and the Impact of Print*[9] how the growing print business destroyed the old practices of polite letters in the 18th Century, and how a new institution, Literature, appeared to replace it by aestheticizing the realities of writing and reading as they were now defined by the marketplace created by printed materials. In Romantic, and subsequently in Modern, literature books were transformed from commodities into great works of art, the labor of writing became creativity, writers were not Grub Street hacks but geniuses, the printed word was endlessly elaborate and infinitely deep, reading was a sacred skill, the content of printed books universal truth. But printways remained the underlying facts of literature.

Not so long ago, this old literature with a capital "L" was a well-established feature in the cultural landscape of the West. By no means so important or solidly institutionalized as the great institutions at the center of society like the law, the state, religion, and the family, literature was still reasonably well-defined and occupied a respectable place in the life of the world. The basic reality of literature was a great tradition of poems, novels, plays, extending from Homer and Virgil, through Dante and Shakespeare, to Goethe, Dickens, Flaubert, and Joyce. This great line of monuments constituting the history of the Western mind, from primitive epics to Eliot's *Waste Land,* was believed to memorialize human creativity, both its origin in the imagination and its form in art, crystalline, perfect, complete, and unchanging, a verbal icon or a well-wrought urn, as two famous images portrayed it. Literature institutionalized the deep workings of the human mind and expressed permanent truths about the human condition in a language of extraordinary power and resonance. It was an ornament to its language and nation, a source of knowledge, a subject worthy of university study and a benefit to all individuals who read it with the care it required and repaid many times over.

By now that *ancien régime* of literature lies in ruins, most unlikely ever to be restored. The forces which brought it down seem from within the institution to be exclusively literary and intellectual, but in the larger social setting in which all print institutions are disintegrating, they have to be considered as the peculiarly literary ways in which electronics pressured this aspect of Gutenberg culture. Over the last twenty years, for example, literary theory pulled down, one by one, all the pillars holding up the old literary temple. Harold Bloom told us that the great writers of the past were the enemies of the belated modern writer, who far from benefiting by standing on the shoulders of his predecessors suffered anxieties of influence until he stepped out from the baleful shadow of earlier poets into the light of his own true self. Geoffrey Hartman declared critics the equals if not the superiors of the poets and novelists. New super-critics dispossessed the authors of the great works of literature past of their literary property and reduced them to "scriptors" who did not create their works, but merely exploited the stock of ideas common to their languages and cultures. Heidegger's "Language writes, not the author" became standard doctrine. Roland Barthes delivered the coup to authors in a famous article, "The Death of the Author," where he wrote that the "author," far from being the creative genius that literature had made him, was only a historical idea "formulated by and appropriate to the social beliefs of democratic, capitalistic society with its emphasis on the individual."[10]

The great literary monuments such as *The Iliad, King Lear, The Brothers Karamazov* that had been thought to exist, like Himalayan peaks, above the hurly-burly of daily life, were declared to be totally political. Virginia Woolf, in "Mr. Bennett and Mrs. Brown," a famous essay printed in 1924, could confidently state that any piece of literature that has some social purpose is not true art since it leaves "one with so strange a feeling of incompleteness and dissatisfaction. In order to complete [it] it seems necessary to do something—to join a society, or more desperately, to write a cheque." But literature has now been so totally politicized that Terry Eagleton tells us that literature is not truth, or even fiction, but "ideology," one of the means "by which certain social groups exercise and maintain power over others."[11]

The most advanced criticism in the last twenty years has been aptly called "a hermeneutics of suspicion" in recognition of its negative approaches to literature. Structuralism "demystified" the literary works by robbing them of their historicity, denying their existence in their own right, and asserting that they had no truth in the sense of referring to reality. Paul de Man warned us, for example, of submitting language "uncritically to the authority of reference.''[12] Deconstruction went on to demonstrate the utter emptiness of literary language, the absence of any meaning whatsoever, or the presence of an infinity of meanings, which comes to the same thing, in the text itself. At the Derridean extreme there isn't anything left to read, in or behind the literary text, only tracks and traces, an infinite regression of deferred realities, each giving a momentary illusion of substance to the other, but eventuating in the void.

Structuralists and deconstructionists have recently responded that far from emptying the texts of meaning, they find more meanings in them than anyone else. But this is true only within that tight little philosophic range within which they operate. For a generation they have relentlessly argued that literary texts always contain the opposite of their apparent meaning, that words do not refer to any external reality, that every seemingly solid proposition rests on nothing more than another proposition, and it in turn on another. It is disingenuous of them, now at a time when their chickens are coming home to roost, to claim that they have shown the way to more and better meanings in the written text, as if they had somehow reinforced the presence of meaning in the text, rather than draining it of its principal sources of authority.

The attacks on literature were not only critical and theoretical. Authority of all kinds has been increasingly suspect since the 1960s, and inevitably the authority of literature's great books was called into question on the social level as well as the theoretical. It seemed outrageous when in 1955 the French anthropologist Claude Lévi-Strauss wrote in *Tristes Tropiques* that ''The primary function of written communication is to facilitate slavery.''[13] But since then the idea that literacy, not illiteracy, has perverted the human spirit has been frequently voiced in numerous ways. The more militant feminists treat the canonical great books as phallocratic expressions of a hegemonic male culture. Marxists and various groups on the cultural left have attacked them as the elitist propaganda of capitalism. One radical Marxist, Louis Althusser, declared the great books to be ''part of the state's ideological apparatus, joining such institutions as the Family, the Church, and the Army in enabling it to reproduce the conditions of its production.''[14] Blacks have denounced the great books as racist. Third-world activists have found literature to be Eurocentric and imperialistic. Gay and lesbian rights groups have seen in the traditional literature the suppression of sexual freedom.

Literature has had few friends in the years when it was being turned topsy-turvy. Books that had until recently been said to be pure art, the ''best that has been thought and said,'' ''the unacknowledged legislation of the world,'' the great treasures of civilization, are now regularly denounced as hegemonic, in bad faith, instruments of a hated repressive political and economic system, the work of ''dead, white males,'' cultural propaganda of the ruling powers on matters of class, gender, and race. By now each and every axiom of the old literature of Romanticism and Modernism—great authors, the permanence and perfection of the literary work of art, truth and complex meaning *in* the works, the beneficent influence of one writer on his successors, the presence of unchanging human truths in the books themselves—has been discredited by iconoclastic criticism and radical social movements. Where not long ago there were what were called "literary works of art"—ordered, teleological, referential, and autonomously meaningful—there are now only what are called "texts," fragmented, contradictory, incomplete, relativistic, arbitrary, and indeterminate. Where intricate meaning was thought to be locked into their structure, they are now treated as a set of broken signs, interpreted with difficulty by readers who try to assemble the fragments into some kind of order. "Oppression studies," "adversary pedagogy," and "cognitive domination" have brought a strident militancy to a literary scene where the armies of structuralism, deconstruction, hermeneutics, feminism, new historicism, Marxism, the Third World, and black and gay studies have swept back and forth over the intellectual battlefield. Nothing remains unquestioned, perhaps nothing remains believable.

One would have expected before the fact that in a time of trial those teachers and critics of literature whose social status and livings depend on literature would have made strong efforts to save as much of the old order as possible. Instead many of them have for twenty years piled on the old literature with such glee and vigor as to force questions about motives. In their own view, of course, they were simply eliminating old error and old injustice in the name of new truth. To their enemies they were merely trendy opportunists. But I want to argue that they have in fact been the unwitting instruments of the same technological forces that have been breaking up other print institutions.

The electronic hand has not so obviously been at work in literature as in the news plant and schoolroom, but it has both directly and indirectly exerted strong pressure. As a result of the ongoing literacy crisis, itself linked to TV, a large number of American colleges and universities have largely ceased to concern themselves with the teaching of literature and have restructured to teach basic writing and reading skills, creative writing, business and technical writing courses. In other places, literary studies have disappeared altogether into on the one hand departments of Cultural Studies, where literature is only one of the many means of structuring consciousness, and on the other into departments of Communications, where the written word is no longer privileged but treated as only one of many media for the storage and dissemination of information.

As what had been the profession of literary study became increasingly a service program, many of those who worked in it were transformed into an intellectual proletariat. Entering the academy in the 1970s and 1980s, they often found themselves part-time teaching help, paid by the hour or the course, without benefits and off the tenure ladder. "Gypsy scholars" who are sometimes paid as little as $400 a course, the number of hours they can teach capped so that the university will not have to pay fringe benefits, are often forced to work at second and third jobs to earn enough to live. No wonder they provided during the 1970s and 1980s a delighted audience for the deconstruction of the old aristocratic literature that had failed to provide them with jobs and status. But as the poor got poorer, professors taught less and less, and more of the teaching was done by the new academic proles. At Berkeley a 1989 walkout of teaching assistants caused the cancellation of 75 per cent of the classes.

Students have responded to the depression in literature by voting with their feet. While the number of bachelor's degrees given in American education overall was increasing by 56 per cent between 1968–1988, degrees in English and other humanities were decreasing by 39 per cent. Only one out of sixteen students now majors in the humanities, where twenty years ago one of six did so. It should be remembered, too, that many enrolled as English majors nowadays are no longer students of literature but of creative, journalistic, and expository writing. Sensitive to the problems in the marketplace, doctoral degrees in literature went down from 1,282 in 1970–1971 to 787 in 1985–1986. In "English and history, the number of doctorates conferred in 1989 was only about half the number conferred just fifteen years earlier," while the numbers in science and engineering were remaining about the same.[15] Men have increasingly avoided the subject as the percentage of women receiving Ph.D.s in literature went from 30 per cent to 66 per cent of the total in the fifteen years 1971–1986.

The Modern Language Association, whose 1992 president is on record that literacy has been socially and personally harmful, has recently mounted a campaign to show that all is much the same as always in the English departments of American universities. No need to get excited! Phyllis Franklin, Executive Director of the Association, points out that the number of B.A.s in English—the other literatures are strangely not mentioned—have been increasing in recent years: "In 1988–89 . . . 33,968 degrees were awarded in English. This is equivalent [equivalent?] to the number granted in 1963–64 and more than twice the number granted in 1955–56."[16] Not only does this ignore the enormous increase in the overall number of B.A.s during those years, it fails to break out the number of bachelor's degrees in writing of various kinds, which steadily increase, from the degrees in literature.

In 1991 the MLA, using a survey of 918 faculty members, with 571 responses (out of a membership of 30,626!), distributed a paper designed to show that the traditional canon was still very much in place and that literature was still taught in much the same way it traditionally had been in American college classrooms. Why they should want to prove that there had been no real change when the more vocal part of their membership, particularly those who run the MLA and speak at the annual convention, are loudly trumpeting a revolution triumphant, it is hard to know. Some residual trace of the old conservative function of the Association, perhaps. But it is hard to read the MLA figures and come to the conclusion that nothing fundamental has changed. "Approximately four-tenths of the respondents [to a question about works thought important for Renaissance literature] regularly teach drama and poetry, the two important literary genres of the period." This is surely putting a "spin" on the figures, for if they don't teach drama and poetry in a Renaissance course, what do the other 60 per cent teach? Bacon and Hobbes, perhaps, but what fills up the rest of the space? Fifty-one per cent of 569 respondents thought that one of the educational goals of their literature courses was to "understand the enduring ideas and values of Western civilization." But 61.7 per cent considered understanding "the influence of race, class, and gender on literature and interpretation" to be of central importance. This represents no substantial change? One could go on in this way, but perhaps the percentages of respondents who thought the following major authors to be "particularly important for 19th-century American literature courses" reveals most clearly what has happened: Hawthorne, 56.3; Thoreau, 49; Melville, 48.4; Emerson, 38.5; Whitman, 28.1; Poe, 8.3; Dickinson, 7.3. That writings which were not formerly canonical are now taught is not surprising, but that half and less of our teachers of American literature don't think our classics important enough to put in their courses surely represents an overwhelming change.

The effects of the electronic revolution appear, less directly but no less surely, I believe, in theory as well as in practice. People who can't read well, or don't need to read very much, are not going to be very interested in the very complicated books and ways of reading that are central to literature. Nor are they likely to continue to accord to printed books and reading the importance that literature has claimed for them in the past. The literacy crisis therefore is a very fundamental threat to literature, and literary theory has, in one way or another, not surprisingly, concentrated its attention in recent years on readers and reading. Of course the theorists of literature are not concerned with the grubby realities of illiterate workers who can't fill out welfare forms and children hunched for eight hours a day in front of the TV. But in the face of a reading problem that threatens literature at its roots, they have come up with a description of the activities of writing and reading that makes it possible for literature to continue to exist in a situation where by the old standards people either read poorly or can't read at all.

Reading, our leading theorists have pronounced, is a very difficult matter. Phenomenological "reader-response" and "reception-aesthetic" types of literary criticism have, for example, characterized the literary texts as incomplete and riddled with gaps, making reading what is called a "problematic" activity, not an exact skill, thus providing room for a multiplicity of interpretations, no one of which is right or "privileged" over any other. Meaning has been diverted from authors and texts to readers, who have been empowered to exercise their own authority in the interpretation of literary texts. Harold Bloom has, by way of epic example, told us of reader-poets who must misread earlier texts to avoid being influenced and deprived of their own authentic voices by their predecessors. Reading badly is, paradoxically, reading well in the world of Bloom. Structuralists have come down for "writerly" over "readerly" texts, books in which readers project their own concerns into the texts rather than subjecting themselves, in the way literate people once did, to an "authoritarian" text and author that determine meaning. Hermeneutics, a general theory of interpretation, posits that meaning is never in the text but always in the theory of interpretation applied to it. Deconstruction, the most radical of the modern literary theories, assumes a basic indeterminacy in all language and a consequent semantic instability in any text, making reading always uncertain and relativistic. At the extreme of this kind of deconstructive criticism, there isn't finally anything there to read, so readers, as the text crumbles before their eyes, can read anything they want into the empty space.

To sum up, authoritarian books and their authors are said to be the trouble, rather than the readers or their teachers. The texts are found to be very hard, incomplete, contradictory, in some ways impossible to read. Ultimately there is nothing in the text to read, so one reading is as good as any other. A multiplicity of meanings is more democratic and more interesting than a set of limited authoritarian meanings imposed by dead authors and canonical texts. To submit to the meaning in the book is to stifle your own authentic self. Reading badly is not just the reality, it is democratically creative. Viewed in the social context of the literacy crisis, structuralism and deconstruction have manufactured an apology for literature which comes down to, "you don't need to be able to read very well to enjoy literature."

Paradoxically, then, "the poetics of illiteracy," as it might with some irony be called, that demystified the old Romantic and Modernist literature can be seen not as the destroyer but as a last-ditch effort in the midst of radical technological change to preserve—even if it meant throwing the baby out with the bath—at least some kind of literature by making reading carefully and accurately unnecessary to literature. Postmodern literary theory offers a fascinating insight into the elaborate and indirect ways in which old institutions respond to threatening technological change without being fully aware of the pressures they are feeling or of how they are responding to the challenges. But the simultaneous appearance of a literacy crisis that threatens literature, and literary theory that concerns itself obsessively with the problems of reading, cannot, I submit, be coincidental.

Here then is my argument. The institutions of the print world are everywhere breaking down, and the literary scandal of the last twenty years is best understood not in the philosophical and political terms in which it offers itself, but as a part of this historical change in communications technology.

Western culture has seen such radical changes in modes of communication before. The Socratic dialogues record the transformation of an oral society into one in which writing began to define truth,[17] and in the 18th Century Alexander Pope described in *The Dunciad* a similar transformation from an old oral-manuscript to a print culture. In this poem, which gave me my first glimpse of how extensive and profound such changes are, Pope correctly foretold that print and the values it encouraged would destroy the old manuscript system of polite letters and help to bring to an end the hierarchical society of which *belles lettres* was a part. He was wrong, however, in his prediction that the triumph of print would restore barbarism and end in a universal darkness in which printer's ink covered all. Print produced a new culture, of which Romantic-Modernist literature was a part, and there is no reason to think that the electronic era will not be similarly inventive and responsive to human needs. But what it produces will be different and may well not have room for a literature of any sort.

Some say, of course, that the disruption is only temporary, or the change only partial, or that the database and CD are only new ways of publishing books, in the end merely more efficient than the scribal manuscript and the printed book. Modems will give us, it is said, entry at last to a complete union catalogue, elaborately cross-indexed, that will provide instant access to all the books ever printed, stored in the super database that will be the library of the future.

But books are very different things from databases and television. Electronic media have already demonstrated that they do not merely modify existing institutions but radically restructure them. In politics, for example, the image has replaced the issue, the very brevity and precision of that conventional *mot* testifying to the absoluteness of the change. The news has been transformed by television into theater, framed and scripted, to provide a thirty-second info byte. Religion increasingly becomes fundamentalist televangelism. The library of postmodernism, the information society's Tower of Babel, already exists, a central database called *Dialogue,* a vast always-growing Info Bank, available full text, on line to subscribers, containing an index to the *New York Times* and several other full-text papers, plus a host of other informational services.

When we look at the transforming power of electronics on society's major institutions, can we doubt that so marginal a print institution as literature will be deeply affected? In a world of xerox, hypertext, and databases, critical literary concepts like copyright, plagiarism, creativity are already becoming vague, and the ambiguities, ironies, and complex structures of thought fostered by printed words are beginning to seem superfluous to audiences accustomed to get their information from TV. Where the fixity of the printed book encouraged the conception of masterworks and permanent human truths, databases and hypertexts in which one thing mixes easily with others and television programs made of images and sounds that flicker past never to be seen or heard again make literary ideas like originality, form, and permanence begin to seem quaint ideas of another age and another people. John Updike, the poet of TV in American life, provides a wonderful picture of how the world appears to a little girl born to TV "flicking silently back and forth between channels" with a remote channel changer: "Faces, black in *The Jeffersons,* white in *Family Ties,* imploringly pop into visibility and then vanish amid shots of beer cans plunged into slow-motion waterfalls, George Bush lugging a gun through Texas underbrush, a Florida farmer gesturing toward his burnt fields, a Scotland Yard detective doing a little lecture with a diagram of an airplane's hold. 'What's he saying?' Harry asks, but even as he asks, the image is gone, replaced by another, of a manatee being implanted with an electronic tracking device by a male pony-tailed manatee-conservation freak. An impatient rage within the child, a gluttony for images, brushes the manatee away."[18]

How will it end? There are apocalyptic *Dunciad* views about. "The growing impoverishment of language will escalate through a series of vicious cycles. Curricula will be streamlined and simplified, and difficult texts will be pruned and glossed. Fewer and fewer people will be able to contend with the masterworks of literature or ideas. Joyce, Woolf, James and the rest will go unread, and the civilizing energies of their prose will circulate aimlessly between closed covers. Whatever exchange of ideas there may have been in our society will wither away except among the echelons of the professional academics. The gulf between the academic and the man on the street, already wide, will become unbridgeable."[19]

On the other hand, there are those who tell us that a postmodernist literature, better than ever and adapted to survive in an electronic era, is already in place—relativistic, democratic, open, political. Literature will now, in this view, be committed to a political program designed to combat the exploitation of people on grounds of race, gender, sexuality, and class. It will reveal the emptiness of language and show how words are used to construct illusions and impose them as ideological realities on individual consciousness. Postmodernist literature, in short, will be a radical, if not an openly revolutionary, subject, dedicated to exposing the fundamental falseness and injustice of society.

For many this appears a brave new world, but in my opinion it is, among its many practical difficulties, caught up in a fatal contradiction. On the one hand it continues to take for granted the importance of the printed text, assuming that books by women and minorities, and deconstructed books that play off the fact that they have no meaning, will continue to retain the traditional authority of the printed word. Will continue to be worth, that is, the laborious reading, the sophisticated interpretation, the frequent reconsideration that the study of literature, however broadly defined, requires. What else are you going to do in the literary classroom if not interpret books? Watch movies? On the other hand, postmodernist literature continues to cut the ground out from under itself by attacking the old books—Homer, Shakespeare, Balzac—showing the emptiness of literary language and texts, how the older works of literature have been used as the instruments of power to establish the ideology of one or another dominant class, demonstrating literature's use in the past wrongfully to suppress the female.

It is the authority of the printed book itself that is in absolute danger, and with it the very existence of a subject based on the idea that the written word is privileged. What is needed at this time if literature in any form is to be salvaged is an effective defense of the book itself, all books, "book-learning," and the first line of that defense surely has to be the remarkable books of the past as well as the present, Aeschylus on justice, Homer on war, Virgil on empire, Dante on the religious spirit, Shakespeare on politics, Dostoevsky on existential choice, Joyce on anomie. We also need, if literature is to survive, to be able to show that the great books of the past and the present offer ways of understanding life and of using language that are unique to the written word and which if lost will truly impoverish our collective ways of thinking about ourselves in contact with the world.

What we say in the defense of literature needs, however, to be plausible. Looking back at the ideas that have legitimated literature in the past, the size of what has characteristically been claimed is startling. Literature is the repetition in the finite mind of the infinite I AM. Poets are the unacknowledged legislators of the world. Literature is the *best* that has been thought and said. Tolstoy could declare that the true artist works "with the awareness of fulfilling the work of God." There is a Wagnerian grandeur to these brags, but given the marginal part that literature and the other arts have actually played in Western society, compared to more central institutions like law or religion, more modest statements might well be more effective.

What we say needs to be helpful as well as plausible. Positive, that is to say, as well as believable. Literary battles in recent years have been violent, and in the heat of battle many things have been said that while they may advance various social causes are definitely not helpful to literature. I would not, for example, class as helpful a statement that a literary text—what we used to call "a work of literature"—means nothing, or means whatever it means to you, any more than I think it helpful to denounce the once-great books that continue to provide the major portion of literature's *raison d'être* as racist, sexist, and elitist.

There are those who would not lament the passing of literature. But for those of us who love the book and want literature in some form or another, however diminished from its past pretensions, to continue to exist, then the time would seem to have come to assert a few very basic literary principles which make it clear to the world what literature is and why it is important.

We need, I think, first of all to define the subject to distinguish it from other kinds of writing, to insist, that is, that there *is* a definable kind of writing we call literature. Most people would agree that literature is distinguished by being self-conscious verbal fiction. There are difficulties with this proposition, as everyone will immediately recognize, such as the fact that literature has historically referred to numerous works from Aelfric's *Homilies* to Boswell's *Life of Johnson* and even perhaps Wordsworth's *Prelude* that are not fiction in the obvious sense of that word. Nor are we likely soon to forget what theory has painfully taught us, that all forms of discourse are fictional in at least some sense. But, still, discussions of literature, in the classroom and in the world, seem, to my ear at least, to assume that literary texts, old or new, differ from other types of texts in being self-consciously aware that they are not trying to be faithful to some prior literal truth. Saying this publicly and consistently would have real advantages. It would define literature's margins, sharply discriminating it from other types of discourse, such as its ancient neighbors, history and philosophy, and it would at the same time claim for it a role of some importance as the manifestation of one of the prime mental faculties, creativity, the ability to make up new realities, and know them as such.

But if we were to say that literature is fiction, which fictions are to be literature? The critical wars of recent years have assured us that the canon will never again be a fixed set of classics. Still, the great majority of literary people want to retain some quality standards for literature. Few are willing to accept, and it would not be helpful to do so, the idea that anything is literature, regardless of how uninteresting or badly written; but they don't want, either, some rigid group of historical texts from a single culture, with some sedimented set of characteristics, to define literature. What has emerged from the critical turmoil of recent years is a deep democratic feeling that the category literature should be genuinely open to the best writing from all places and all times, with the further understanding that what is considered "best" is not inscribed in stone but will change as circumstances change. Most immediately this means that our traditional emphasis on English literature, which has long condemned American writing to a subordinate role and forced American culture to play the part of a vulgar Rome to Britain's sophisticated Athens, ought to be a thing of the past. "Literature," not English, French, Italian, Russian, or Latin American and all the other national literatures, is what really interests most writers and critics nowadays, and literature would be greatly strengthened if we were to begin openly to speak and teach along these lines, without regard for the nationality, race, sex, or class of the writer.

Thirdly, it seems to me that the theories of recent years declaring the emptiness of literary language and the total dependence of a text for its meaning on the reader have earned literature a foolish name in the world, without the idea ever being fully believed within literature itself. At the high philosophical level, these theories of the emptiness of the text, or of an infinity of potential meanings, are logically demonstrable, as is the more serious view that the words are ultimately meaningless because they do not refer to any reality outside the language. "There is nothing outside text." But at the practical level, writers and readers of literature, including its teachers, still assume, because they really have no alternative, that writers use words to say something to their readers and that, within reason—the governing term is "within reason"—that meaning, which it is possible to get, roughly, wrong or right, is *in* the text. Equally importantly, if literature is to have any importance in the world, it must refer to realities outside itself, and this almost all who write and teach it still assume. Deconstruction exposed the excesses of the old formalist New Criticism that located its own super-refined meanings in the text itself, and various kinds of reader-response criticism have made clear the involvement of readers in the construction of meaning. But to accept in practice that there is no meaning in literature's words except what we impute to them is not really a tenable working position, and reviews, quite properly, go on telling us what books have to say, while the great majority of classrooms pursue some kind of general meaning in *Hamlet* or in the latest novel of Don DeLillo or Joyce Carol Oates, both of whom are happy to tell you *what they wrote*. Whatever its shock value, literature would profit enormously by getting rid of what almost no one really believes anyway, that there is no meaning *in* the text, or that it refers to nothing outside the text, and offering itself once again as a particular literary way of making statements and understanding human beings in their world.

Finally, it seems to me crucial that we begin collectively to assert again, what most of us willy-nilly act upon, that the texts we call literature are beneficial, not harmful, to individuals and society. Not long ago literature was generally assumed to be the *best* that had been thought and said, and while there is no chance of returning to that lost innocence, proving that it is the *worst* is neither a plausible nor helpful activity. At times in the recent past, the more radical literary critics seem to have been bent on destroying literature. Marxists declared that the printed word lied in numerous ways to serve the interests of ruling class and the state. "Intellectual freedom fighters" spoke of literature as an instrument of oppression, furthering imperialism and colonialism. Feminists told us that literature has excluded women and served the cause of male dominance. It is difficult to see how in the long run literature that has been stripped in this systematic way of any positive value, has been declared so harmful to the cause of human freedom and understanding, can be considered worth teaching and reading.

The Gutenberg Era is gone, and with it the old literature's authors of imaginative genius and their crystalline works of perfect art and unchanging truth, the great march down the centuries—Homer, Shakespeare, Balzac. Books themselves are becoming culturally marginal, and if a book-based institution like literature is to survive in some form, positive ways to speak of it must be found again. It will no longer do, in my opinion, to go on saying that the language of the texts is empty, or to treat them as bastions of male supremacy, or the propaganda of long-dead tyrannies, or the ideology of power designed to tighten the chains privilege loads on the poor, the ignorant, and the helpless. "Why bother to read or teach such pernicious stuff?" is the question the world is already asking and will ask more and more as electronic media increasingly supply more information and amusement. Of course, we can simply let literature go, and it may well disappear no matter what we do, but if we want to preserve some kind of literature, however culturally marginal it may become, then the time is short in which to begin saying plausible and helpful things about it.

NOTES

1. Humphrey Carpenter, *A Serious Character: The Life of Ezra Pound* (Boston: Houghton/Miflin, 1988), p. 913.

2. Anthony Smith, *Goodbye Gutenberg: The Newspaper Revolution of the 1980s* (Oxford: Oxford University Press, 1980), p. 236.

3. Yale University Council Committee on the Library. Unpublished report of May, 1987.

4. *New York Times* (June 3, 1991), B6.

5. Tony Rothman, "Reader Rip-Off," *New Republic* (February 3, 1992), p. 14.

6. Roger Cohen, "In re: Marketing Parameters for Great American Novel," *New York Times* (March 25, 1990), E5.

7. *New Republic* (June 17, 1991), p. 16.

8. George Packer, "The Struggling Writer: Gissing Had It Right," *New York Times Book Review* (October 13, 1991), p. 29.

9. Princeton: Princeton University Press, 1987.

10. "The Death of the Author," in *Image, Music, Text,* trans. Stephen Heath (Glasgow: Fontana/Collins, 1977), p. 142.

11. *Literary Theory: An Introduction* (Oxford: Oxford University Press, 1983), p. 42.

12. Paul de Man, "Semiology and Rhetoric," in *Textual Strategies: Perspectives in Post-Structuralist Criticism,* ed. Josué V. Harari (Ithaca: Cornell University Press, 1979), p. 121.

13. Trans. John and Doreen Weightman (New York: Atheneum, 1974), p. 299.

14. Louis Althusser, "Ideology and Ideological State Apparatuses (Notes Towards an Investigation)," in *Lenin and Philosophy and Other Essays,* trans. Ben Brewster (New York: Monthly Review Press, 1971), p. 156.

15. William G. Bowen and Neil L. Rudenstine, *In Pursuit of the Ph.D.* (Princeton: Princeton University Press, 1992), p. 26.

16. Letter, *Princeton Alumni Weekly* (Feb. 19, 1992), p. 2.

17. For the authoritative discussion of this event see Eric Havelock, *A Preface to Plato* (Cambridge, Mass.: Harvard University Press, 1963).

18. *Rabbit at Rest* (New York: Ballantine Books, 1990).

19. Sven Birkerts, "Crisis in Literature," *Chronicle of Higher Education* (September 25, 1991), B6.

2.

The Canon and the Classroom: A Caveat

LESLIE A. FIEDLER

As I was pondering what I might usefully say about the future of literary studies in English—especially its role in establishing and maintaining a canon (which has become, for better or worse, one of its chief functions)—I received a rather disconcerting dispatch from that future. There arrived on my desk, that is to say, a letter from my granddaughter detailing the curriculum in a summer seminar for gifted high school seniors, intended to prepare them, I suppose, not just for college but, in some cases at least, careers as teachers of English. Delighted to have been so honored, she was even more delighted by what she was learning. "Wonderful," she called her courses, which included (all too predictably), "Ideology in Children's Literature," "Black English," "Post-Modernist Theatre," and "Feminist Poetry." Then she concluded by writing, "I feel as if a whole new world is opening up to me"; to which I found myself responding (an improbable Prospero in Buffalo, New York), " 'Tis new to thee."

It was not merely the cant words in the course titles which dismayed me (I am allergic to all words ending in "-ism," particularly those I have been tempted on occasion to use myself), but my sense that I had lived through all of this before, trapped in a half-century-long bad dream. Over and over again, I have watched a presumable critical breakthrough, an opening up of new insights tend first to turn into a fad, then a cliché; and finally on the level of day-to-day pedagogy become a canon, enforced in the totalitarian regime of the classroom, where whatever is not required is forbidden.

I have, indeed, long considered it my special function in the academy to combat that all but inevitable tendency; beginning before I even suspected that I myself might someday end up as an academic expected to impose what was currently canonical in quest of promotion, tenure, and the respect of my colleagues. I can remember, for instance, rising in my high school sophomore English class (from whose walls portraits of the Boston Brahmins looked down in silent disapproval) to protest that our poetic horizons should not be bounded by those genteel New England Sages. Nor, I insisted with all the arrogance of youth, should our novel-reading be confined to *Ivanhoe, Silas Marner,* and *The Virginian*—a list chosen for us by a committee of college professors, most of them long dead.

Even in Graduate School I still found it necessary to continue to fight the good fight, this time against living Professors, who thought of themselves as emancipated from the timidity and sentimentality of late Victorianism, but as "historical scholars" found any work published after the mid-nineteenth century (especially, it turned out, American books) unworthy of serious study. But—as I could not resist pointing out—even the canon of the centuries they deigned to treat in learned articles was being changed at the moment by the more recent authors they chose to ignore. John Donne, for instance, was coming to be prized more highly than Milton and Gerard Manley Hopkins, more esteemed than Tennyson or Browning; even as Hawthorne and Melville were threatening to replace Dickens and Thackeray in the pantheon of great novelists.

It was, of course, the pioneers of High Modernism and the "New Critics" who canonized them who inspired me. I had been reading Proust and Joyce behind my timid teachers' backs since the age of thirteen; and by the time I came of legal age, I had not merely begun my lifelong love-hate relationship with Ezra Pound and T.S. Eliot but had already discovered Charles Olson in the pages of an obscure little magazine. I had, moreover, been influenced by critical revisionists like John Crowe Ransom, Allen Tate, and F.R. Leavis. It was they who first awoke in me the hope of creating a kind of meta-canon without limits and forever changing; thus making it possible for the study and even the teaching of literature to become more like literature itself: not an act of conformity and submission to established authority, but a way of challenging and subverting the *status quo* whatever it might be—a way of saying "No! in thunder."

The epigones of Modernism, however, ended by destroying one rigid canon only to create another. At their worst, they defined, like F.R. Leavis, a "great tradition" so narrow that it excluded such long-established classics as *Jane Eyre, Wuthering Heights,* and *Tristram Shandy.* But even at their more generous best, they consigned to the outer darkness many books which had pleased many and pleased long—on the grounds that precisely because they had done so they had proved themselves unredeemable trash. Moreover, such critics had trouble coming to terms with borderline writers, including some who had been my own favorites. I am thinking in particular of Walt Whitman, who theoretically at least wrote for the popular audience;

Edgar Allan Poe, who wooed—and eventually won—that audience, though he boasted of spurning it; and especially Harriet Beecher Stowe, who not merely aspired to best-sellerdom but achieved it.

In the two critical works which established the Modernist canon for American Literature, Matthiessen's *American Renaissance* and Lawrence's *Studies in Classic American Literature, Uncle Tom's Cabin* was completely ignored. But this was predictable enough, was it not?; since Nathaniel Hawthorne, a special favorite of both Matthiessen and Lawrence, seems to have been thinking chiefly of Mrs. Stowe when he excoriated "the damned female scribblers," against whom, he thought, he and other more serious writers (all male, of course) had to contend for readers. In my own *Love and Death in the American Novel* I tacitly accepted the Matthiessen-Lawrence canon; but over the next decade I become more and more ill at ease with the odd blending of snobbism and misogyny which had prompted Mrs. Stowe's exclusion.

It was not, however, until the publication of *What Was Literature?* that I publicly called for opening up the canon to include her—along with Alex Haley, Thomas Dixon, Jr., and Margaret Mitchell, whose *Gone with the Wind* has finally outsold even *Uncle Tom's Cabin,* becoming simultaneously the most widely sold and loved and the most critically despised of American books. In large part because of this, my last full-length critical study has become, ironically enough, the least widely sold and loved of all my own books; most vilified, of course, by certain last-ditch defenders of High Modernism as Hugh Kenner, a political as well as aesthetic reactionary, and therefore particularly offended by my shameless populism.

I was not utterly dismayed, however, since Modernism was already obsolescent, if not quite obsolete. Indeed, its successors had already appeared, new aspirants to new canon-making. One wing of the so-called post-Modernists (I was one of the first to call them by that now much abused name), for instance, declared their intent to close the gap which the Modernists had widened between High Art and Pop. They argued, as I myself had done much earlier, that the true mythology of the late twentieth century was to be found in the fast foods rather than the *haute cuisine* of contemporary literature; and, in fact, some among them larded their experimental novels with allusions to and downright emulation of science fiction, comic books, and Class-B horror movies. But did this not mean, I found myself asking, opening the canon, the classroom curriculum to such works, including even the commodity novels of shameless schlock artists like Stephen King?

That the most admired post-Modernist novelists of our time thought no such thing, I found out rather painfully when I was moved to observe toward the end of a conference attended by many of them that King's books might still be read and cherished when the experimental fiction we ourselves wrote had long been forgotten. *Misery,* I suggested, might well turn out to be for the eighties and nineties what *Gone with the Wind* had been for the thirties: a reproach to critics, indeed, to any presumptuous making of canons. My remarks, however, stirred no assent, not even embarrassed laughter. Instead, I was greeted with a hushed silence, as if I had committed some unspeakable sacrilege; and I was assigned to the equivalent of the children's table at the ceremonial banquet which concluded our sessions.

But this should not have surprised me, since I had long since become uncomfortably aware that even in their essays written in praise of Pop the post-Modernists had used the hermetic jargon invented by elite French critics, bent on undermining the authority of primary texts and the autonomy of their authors. Unlike most eminent Anglo-American critics, such ideologues were not themselves creative writers attuned to a larger audience; and consequently they wrote in a language incomprehensible to any but their academic colleagues—plus, of course, their students who aspired to a similar status. I began, therefore, to look in another direction for possible allies in my quest to redeem the teaching of English by inventing a new canon more congruous with the values of an open society and the writers of song and story, from Sophocles and Shakespeare to Dickens, Twain, and Mrs. Stowe, who had pleased its mass readership, whether or not they had passed critical muster.

In *What Was Literature?,* I had contended that this breaking down the boundaries between High Art and Pop would enable us to read without prejudice hitherto despised works by underprivileged groups in our society: women; Black Americans; Native Americans; homosexuals; Hispanics; even Rednecks, the "niggers" of the presumably enlightened. Such works had been underesteemed, it seemed to me, because the earlier makers of our canon had been chiefly college-educated, straight WASP males, who (speaking only to each other) had found it possible to identify their parochial prejudices with universal aesthetic standards. With this diagnosis of our cultural plight, militant feminists, gays, Indians, and Afro-Americans seemed at first sight to agree.

They, too, however, turned out to be untrustworthy allies—finally, only another kind of enemy. To begin with, some of them, though dedicated to opening up the canon in terms of gender and race, still smuggled in the old elitist distinctions of High and Low. A recent highly respected history of African-American literature, for instance (its author himself black), not only ignores a street writer like Iceberg Slim, but passes over in silence Frank Yerby, the most widely read author of his race; and does not even mention the immensely talented Samuel Delany—presumably because his books, marketed as science fiction, are, whatever their intrinsic merits, generically extra-canonical.

Even more disconcertingly, such "progressive" revisers of the canon end by excluding as well as including works on ideological grounds; so that their new canon is finally even narrower than the reactionary one they began by deploring. On the one hand, they urge teaching works written by members of previously underesteemed groups in our society, along with those written by anyone which present what are considered at the moment in liberal academic circles correct views on ethnicity, sexuality, age, and physical impairment. Yet at the same time, and on the same high moral/political grounds, they urge dropping from our curriculum books which support views on the subjects with which they happen at that moment to disagree, labeling them "racist," "sexist," "ageist," "homophobic," etc. etc. The more fanatic and finicky among them even consider the use of the customary colloquial derogatory names for embattled minorities sufficient grounds for snatching books from the hands of students. But it is notoriously hard to keep up with such lexical orthodoxy. "Darky" and "coon," much less "nigger," have long been deemed dirty words by the "enlightened"; but more recently "negro" has become suspect and even "Afro-American" not quite kosher enough.

Worst of all, though, is the demand of some ardent multiculturalists for the proportional representation in the canon of hitherto excluded minorities. Certainly, the drive to include a percentage of, say, Native and African-American novelists and poets equal to what their people make up in the total population has proved a total disaster in our polyethnic United States; since it has led to exclusion of certain writers who have pleased many and pleased long, simply because they happen to be "DWEMs." "Dead White European Males," however, happen to have written most of the books read and loved by such minorities once they have attained literacy. Moreover, these former oppressors have also invented the genres in which the formerly oppressed are presently seeking to render their unique experiences.

Please understand, when I speak of the calamitous resolutes of such misguided book-banning, I am not just thinking of the lunatic political fringe which annually calls for keeping a "racist" *Huckleberry Finn* out of the classroom. Much less am I referring to the yahoos who picket with equal self-righteousness campus buildings where *The Birth of a Nation* is being shown and those in which courses in the Great Books of Western Civilization are being taught. Such protestors are the victims of their own ignorance. Not only are they incapable of reading books or films in any way but ideologically; they are also unaware that the so-called "Western Civilization" has always been multicultural.

In its centuries of imperialist expansion the West, even as it has sought to impose some of its own values of alien cultures it has encountered, has simultaneously assimilated theirs. So Longfellow sought to render Native-American legend in the meter of Finnish epic, at the same historical moment that Thoreau and Whitman and Emerson were attempting to make Persian and Hindu myth available to the world of middle-class WASPs. Nor did the process cease in the age of High Modernism, when Ezra Pound dedicated himself to re-imagining contemporary experience in terms of Zen poetry and Confucian philosophy; while at the same time Picasso was learning from African sculpture new ways to see and render the human face.

But this was only to be expected; since from its very beginnings Western culture was rooted in many cultures. It was born, after all, in the eastern Mediterranean, where the Middle East and Europe, Hebraism and Hellenism, the Semitic and Japhetic merge. But Hamitic elements were present from the start, too. Not only did the Greeks learn much from the Egyptians, but writers whom we think of as belonging to a world dominated by Greece and Rome were in fact Africans: Aesop, for instance, and Apuleius, Terence, and Saint Augustine. Moreover, even after the invention of nationalist Europe, such canonical writers as Dumas and Pushkin were of African descent. To be sure, they made it into the canon—in this respect, quite like Europeanized Jews, from Spinoza and Heine to Proust and Kafka— not because of their alien ethnic origin, but in bland disregard of that fact.

No, it is not the rabid racist "anti-racists" who disturb me finally. It is rather the well-intentioned and knowledgeable young people, misled by (alas, only half-understood) attempts at opening the canon, including my own. I have just learned, for instance, that the most recently hired young instructor at a private secondary school where my wife teaches in his proposed list of readings for an introductory course in American Literature did not include a single book by Hawthorne, Melville, Twain, Hemingway, or Faulkner. But, of course, women and African-American writers—most of lesser distinction—were dutifully included. He was, of course, only trying to be "politically correct," as that term is defined by the liberal academic establishment; yet in doing so he was—perhaps unwittingly—collaborating in the creation of what may well be the most totalitarian of all canons. Not merely is it as narrow as the Modernist canon which preceded it; but, unlike the latter, it is immune to criticism in the sense that anyone who objects to it is morally suspect. That is to say, it is based not on aesthetic standards, about which men of goodwill can disagree; it rests rather on ideological and ethical values, which its advocates believe to be not just something to which they happen to subscribe at the moment but one valued for all times and places, *right* forever.

Confusingly, however, many of those who are opposed to Political Correctness are equally sure that their notions about what the "Western Tradition" is—and therefore what the canon should be—are eternally right. In support of their contention they claim a direct line of descent from Plato and Sophocles; though, in fact, their genteel standards date back no further than Queen Victoria and the Boston Brahmins. Similarly, their opponents would have us believe that their ideological approach is rooted in the teachings of those anti-Victorian Victorians, Marx and Engels; though their rhetoric smacks more of the Fireside chats of Franklin Delano Roosevelt. The current debate about the canon seems, therefore, not a confrontation between eternal verities, but an extension of the journalistic debate between left-wing Democrats and right-wing Republicans. This is only to be expected, in any case, since an overwhelming majority of the elite academic community tends to support the former, while an equal percentage of extra-academic middle Americans continues stubbornly to vote for the latter.

Consequently, most of the spokesmen for the recent backlash against "multiculturalism" are politicians and bureaucrats elevated to power in the Reagan-Bush administrations, plus a handful of hard-line conservative newspaper columnists, whose highest ambition is to be reprinted in *Reader's Digest*. But they include also elitist college professors like Allan Bloom, whose reactionary *Closing of the American Mind* (with an approving introduction by the Nobel Laureate, Saul Bellow) had already become a best-seller even before the current pedagogical debate had been reduced to journalistic platitudes. The readership of that ill-tempered diatribe did not consist mainly of arrant yahoos, but included some who buy books and may even read them: primarily, I assume, college-educated parents of the students we are currently teaching.

Like Bloom himself, they may have been permanently traumatized by the cultural revolution of the sixties; and they are therefore profoundly disturbed to discover their children being taught by survivors of those troubled times, now tenured and aging, but dedicated still to the subversive values they then espoused. But surely, such parents end by thinking, if everything such "progressive" teachers teach is wrong, wrong, wrong— everything in the tradition they deny (and which Bloom supports) must be right, right, right—and should therefore be not merely advocated but enforced.

Such self-righteous yea-sayers agree with their self-lefteous opponents on only one thing: that not to choose between them, not to take sides is the ultimate betrayal of culture. I, alas, find little or nothing to choose; but how to say so and be heard has long been and remains for me still a problem. Initially, I thought it would be sufficient simply to keep on repeating the cryptic phrase of Melville's which I have made my *leitmotif* throughout my writing career: "All men who say yes lie. . . ." I feared, though, that those I addressed, contemptuous of ambivalence and unprepared to admit that all things—even our most dearly held pieties—change with time, would not listen. And so I ended up repeating in the silence of my troubled head (what I at long last say aloud here) the wish I once heard William Burroughs express: that a toxin might be invented which would destroy all those who think they are right.

It occurs to me, however, as I prepare to conclude, that there is such a toxin, namely, literature itself. To be sure, on the didactic or ideological level, song and story may seem to confirm the values of the social groups by whom and for whom it is written, thus preserving the status quo. But on deeper archetypal levels (and all literature which survives its historical moment is rooted in archetypes), it prepares for change by expressing the otherwise unconfessed dark side of our ambivalence: chiefly our hatred and fear of the Other. That Other is, though customarily defined in terms of race, gender, generation, or class, a projection of all that is unredeemably alien in the depths of our own psyches.

It is for this reason that the books we teach will deliver us (at least so I assure myself) not just from the fashionable methodologies with which we approach them and the currently fashionable canonical distinctions we vainly seek to impose; but finally from the temptation to believe that—unlike our deluded predecessors—we have at long last really got it *right*.

3.

English as Something Else

GEOFFREY HARTMAN

When the English Institute begins to talk about Institutions, is there cause for alarm? Fifty years is lifetime enough for an institute—though not, of course, for an institution like Church or State, which used to be honored by the adjective "divine." Can we trust institutes over fifty?

There were giants in those days: when William Wimsatt, Jr. rose to speak, his towering stature acted as demeanor evidence. I felt like Jack in the Beanstalk. We too are a colorful bunch, yet more chaotic, that is pluralistic, more self-affirming in our negations, speaking in tongues or idiolects, and reaching—I believe—a higher level of enjoyment, even if it is that of a *société du spectacle.* After half-a-century we may even be developing a sense of humor. "Masterpiece Theater" by Gilbert and Gubar Productions is as much to the point as Steve Martin in *Three Amigos,* when he shows his Hollywood buddies a bullet like the one that has just wounded him, and says unbelievingly: "It's real, fellas!"

Reality in America has always been a perplexing subject for the culture critic. Promised land and Wasteland converge. America lacked, Henry James alleged in his essay on Hawthorne, "items of high civilization." Writers had to find their symbols and institutions in a world elsewhere, and perhaps create that world. The situation today is not different but has spread globally. We shuttle between a sense of un- and surreality. All our cultural hopes and schemes, all our progressive expectations, have not brought justice about. This "poverty of philosophy" stands in strange contrast to a luxury of choices in the multicultural marketplace (its items of both high and low culture, its lifestyles, voices, even identities). An excess embarrasses the choosing: what sanctions this rather than that?

Baudrillard explains the phantom surplus by saying that only reruns are left after modernity's liberating orgy and technology's power of instant communication.[1] This sounds suspiciously like an older form of culture-pessimism, denying the possibility of creative life after the Classics. To Baudrillard I prefer William James's vision of "a lot of eaches . . . in no wise short-circuited by some essential oneness."[2] "I prefer"? A personalistic and disarming phrase evades the issue of *el vertigo del entre* (Octavio Paz).

The English Institute changed radically from the late sixties on, turning first toward literary studies as an interdisciplinary whole, then toward art as social text. We all feel we have gained by that. But has there also been a loss?

There is a growing awareness that the expansion has not prevented a new constriction. To open the curriculum is one thing; to justify or evaluate what passes through is another. There are only so many books one can read intensively; if we had to make a reasoned choice among all competitors, we would spend our time entirely in reasoning rather than reading. What we call the canon are those works we start reading straightaway, with the expectation that they will prove their worth. Even today, then, we are tempted to invest in a canon and to construct a lasting rationale. This rationale has become explicitly ideological: a choice is often made on social and restitutive grounds.

Despite appearances to the contrary, this means that the grounds of decision are often narrowly construed. We still forgive Mozart's *Magic Flute* despite its benighted view of women, but for how long? Will we have to disqualify the Gospels because of their anti-Jewish polemics? Must we avert our eyes from Picasso's "The Artist and his Model" series because it is bullish about the male? An extreme is the Rushdie case, a nightmare that looms when ideological purity combines with political clout.

A social choice criterion may ultimately have a narrowing effect on knowledge. It can be justified provisionally if it helps to motivate learning about a heritage that has been suppressed or neglected. Then, like the field of comparative literature, but with a larger-than-European focus, or one different from it, the text-milieu expands. This expansion does not guarantee a qualitative "reading" of all those cultural texts. It simply sets the stage, as historicism did, with its fraternal axiom that all nations are equally near to God. To pass from acknowledgment to knowledge is the hard thing. It requires, once more, some choice between competing curricular options— options that can become demands when politicized.

There is, in short, a vertigo of choice, coming from our cultural relativism; and it is often resolved today by deciding what will sustain a community that is finding its voice, that is creating or recreating itself. The relation between critic and audience becomes, then, a relation between critic and community; perhaps this has always been the case. To be part of that community and yet to be a critic, raises the stakes.[3] It is disappointing to hear the claim, surely a simplifying one, that we are somehow more expert in dealing with opposition, difference, and otherness. The good intention matters but less than the quality of the consent we give or urge. A programmatic intimacy will shortcircuit reading as much as outright antagonism does.

The relation of criticism to quality of consent in an era of progressive politics deserves more attention. Freedom of choice often results in a compulsive search for identity and commitment. Public opinion and peer pressure take on more not less importance. Those who dissent from a culture perceived as dominant and repressive will at some point assent to a different one. Democracy does not resolve that issue but makes it fully conscious. "In our times," John Stuart Mill said in *On Liberty,* "from the highest class of society down to the lowest, every one lives under the eye of a hostile and dreaded censorship." He meant the pressure to conform, until "by dint of not following their own nature [people] have no nature to follow." The result, paradoxically, is the negation of that personal development encouraged by democracies. We "become incapable of any strong wishes or native pleasures, and are generally without either opinions or feelings of home growth." Mill ends: "Now is this, or is it not, the desirable condition?"

Undesirable, of course; yet Stanley Cavell has suggested that Mill's question must nevertheless remain a question. The answer may be obvious yet Mill does not denounce herd democracy as Nietzsche might have done, or tout inconsistency in Emerson's impish manner. If the critical issue is individualism, its possibility in a democratic-political context, then, as Cavell remarks, the "implication seems to be that until we each give our answers to the question, one by one, one on one, we will not know what it is to which we are giving our consent."

Put it this way: there are surprises in thought and language, not just in politics. As critics we call a text into question; but often that "call" has already come from a text that questions us. An unexpected and successful move in chess is recorded by the addition of an !, and that is the feeling we get from great writers too, not always at first, but when—perhaps with the aid of critics and expositors—we follow their meaning. Our apathy or supersophistication is breached by a moment of woe and wonder: wonder at the creative couth of the writer, woe that we seem so untalented in comparison. Our admiration for such work, then, rarely stems from a particular message or preachment. However exemplary we feel the work to be, there is both a sensual and a consensual element that must be taken in and does not yield to precept or command. The consumer—the person at the receiving end—is made active in the very act of receiving, of attending specifically to the language, the texture, the formal properties of the statement.

This attentiveness is the critic's due process, a respect for otherness and the encouragement of time for thought. It enables the build-up of enough reflective pressure to isolate false originality (the flashy shortcuts of newsspeak) and false traditionality (the comfortable clichés of academic or bureaucratic jargon). Language speaks to us in ways more complex than water carries a swimmer: when Valéry said of Mallarmé that he used language as if he had invented it, he paid his predecessor a supreme compliment, knowing how impossible it was to achieve such insight or control. What the critic aims for, similarly, is "counter-love, original response" (Frost) rather than a language above language claiming scientific or moral truth.

Allow me now to tell a story in the form of a historical retrospect. In a way it remains a political story. In the England of the 1920s the appreciation of literature was made somewhat less dependent on social class by instituting a university course of study. This effort raised two questions still relevant to us. First: could English become an institution, that is, a scholarly field in the university, without succumbing to false rigor and pedantry? Then, the obverse of that: could English overcome the doubt—mainly from the side of science and philosophy—that it would always be the province of dilettantes?

Students went to Oxbridge to "read"; but I.A. Richards found that reading had first to be learned. Focusing less on what was read than on the ability to interpret and judge what was read, his *Practical Criticism* of 1929 recorded student responses to unidentified poems. The dismal result showed that "reading" was mostly a way of foreclosing meaning by applying clichés and confirming the standard culture. In his earlier book, *Principles of Literary Criticism* (1924), Richards had already set out to improve reading through teachable principles (the word "institutions" would have seemed inflated) that bypassed antiquarian, jingoistic, and snobbish interests.

While the issue of subcultures and identity-construction did not arise, moral and technical matters combined in interestingly messy ways. (The word "principles" itself had a moral as well as scientific ring.) Richards's concern was for the culture as a whole: the reintegration of scientific, poetic, and moral thought. In this pursuit of a unified sensibility he resembled Eliot, but his aim was perhaps more ambitious, namely, to reconcile *paideia* and public education. Literature "read aright" could help to rectify a psychic and cultural disequilibrium, until the creative and analytic aspects of our nature, overformalized as art and science, would show once more a measure of mutuality. A Greek ideal of balance survives here in modern dress.

At present we are troubled by the failure of this project. The ethos of integration on which it was based could not keep up with the task of assimilating modern experience and social change. A new ethos of diversity and multiculturalism has taken hold. But this achievement will be in vain if reading is jeopardized as a disciplined and imaginative form of life. Today the appreciation of literature is clearly less prejudiced or class-bound than before;[4] and the energy of debate, and sometimes of intellect, has soared. Literature *has* achieved integrity as a university subject. Yet one doubt will not go away: is there something about literary study that remains intractably ideological, so that it can never attain the rigor of philosophy or science?[5]

The quest for a "science of literature," so important on the Continent after Saussure and Jakobson, reached America in the 1960s and produced remarkably precise and fascinating work. Literary theory became a subject of discussion and dispute. But theory, as in Wellek and Warren, could simply mean literary study methodically freeing itself of nationalistic or other non-literary motives. There is, however, a purer type of theory that breaks with empirical motives and substitutes linguistic terms for historical, psychological, or aesthetic ones in literary analysis.[6] This development comes after Richards and does not achieve true momentum until the advent of semiology, structuralism, and deconstruction.

A resistance to theory of this purer kind is heightened by the fact that the theory shifts attention away from "reading aright," or the discovery of a meaningful intention (ethical, historical, aesthetic), toward language as a medium that can never be as transparently communicative as the word "intention" suggests. Literature as the object of theory is best described, rather, in categories derived from rhetoric and poetics. Hermeneutic and historical perspectives can also enter but may not hierarchically preempt theory's linguistic turn. De Man acknowledges that this methodological shift is unlikely to be generally adopted. For it would change, he says ironically, "departments of English from being large organizations in the service of everything except their own subject matter. . . ."[7] Indeed, a conflict about what reading is has developed: Common Readers (to use a traditional phrase) and theory-conscious readers split into separate and often hostile factions.[8]

It is not science, then, but a moral or communitarian concern that challenges literary theory today. Ethics bounces back from its discredited status as cerebral or even hypocritical. This return to ethics or "vital reason" is familiar enough after the Enlightenment. Consider only that Nietzsche's transvaluation of values begins with an attack on "theoretical man" for finding the "highest satisfaction in the unveiling process itself"—and gloating about it. Nietzsche's critique of the overvalued intellect (in *Birth of Tragedy,* section 15, he blames Socrates for starting us down that road) is but one of many anti-self-consciousness polemics that anticipate our own anti-theory concerns as well as the struggle for a more dialogical ethics in Buber, Rosenzweig, and Levinas.[9]

The good news, then, is that literary studies have experienced an epoch of expansion, as Arnold would have called it, for well over half-a-century. Despite the vicissitudes of action and reaction, the thinkers alluded to have made our field more outgoing, more inclusive, more principled in its claims, more precise in its presentational methods, more heuristic in spirit and transnational in orientation. Though they stumbled often enough by confusing pedagogical and evangelical motives, they rarely lost sight of the literary text. The bad news is that while so much energy goes into expanding the reading list, we forget that it is skilled reading that expands it, that film, and material or popular culture, become in that way part of our text-milieu—become texts even when they are, say, images—and that this skill used to be honed by literature. But now the literary text seems to fade into the social text. The expansion is being driven less by critical reading than by the manifest content of a work or the sociological *bona fides* of its author. English has become something else.

Yet was English ever itself? Like so many academic fields it was conceived in ideology. It favored English English, marginalized a "Commonwealth of Letters," established a postclassical canon of its own, giving Moderns and Modernists parity with the Ancients, and rejected the German University's separation of criticism, deprecated as belletristic, from philology, proclaimed to be *wissenschaftlich*. And though the Cambridge "School of English," founded after the Great War, cannot be identified with its influential gadfly, F.R. Leavis, his obstinacy in limiting curricular study to English writers in a Great Tradition fostered a parish mentality, a Church (albeit dissenting) within the University.[10]

Being conceived in ideology is not as fatal, however, as original sin. There is room for a self-generated grace, for development beyond this moment of origin. Close reading, brilliantly staged by Empson, survives to this day as a presentational device that keeps the text central without overobjectifying it. Quotations become fragments as well as illustrations; they are extracts representing the work but also free the reader's imagination toward multivocal options, the making of meaning and a precarious linguistics of transmission.

The technique, in fact, maintained a delicate balance between the older "moral sciences" (formerly *Geisteswissenschaften*) and the emerging field of the social sciences. To read Empson and Richards—or, in America, Burke and Blackmur—is to find oneself in the presence of an intelligence that will not give up personal testimony for a stricter language of proofs. Theirs remains an open-ended discourse: impressions are erected into contingent truths rather than laws.[11]

This type of literary study proved immensely attractive to many in graduate school after World War II. Practical criticism seemed moral enough in its care for words and distrust of slogans: it was too soon after Stalinist and Nazi appropriations of culture to attempt an institutional format based on political or scientific coordinates. The impact on the humanities of racial and cultural politics showed itself less as ideology-critique than as ideology-avoidance. The covert Christianity of much American New Criticism also escaped analysis.

This phase of organized innocence allowed the field to recuperate and expand in both scholarly and pedagogical directions. Reading Northrop Frye we did not think about Spengler, although something of the latter's cultural morphology (that caffeine of the intellectuals) remained. And when we studied Curtius, the issue of Latinity, or whether French civilization was reconcilable with German culture, did not come up. Moreover, had we realized how many French authors harbored a sympathy for fascism, it might have been impossible to avoid a political test that would have discredited some of the most famous.

As in Trilling, there was a shift to politics in "the wide sense of the word," or toward culture as the larger, the more generous and subsuming, category. Trilling helped to bring literature into the university as the best object for cultural criticism. Yet he wondered whether *modern* works, focused on extremity, were teachable.[12] A hermeneutic doubt (can what is alien or other be understood?) returned as a pedagogical scruple during the time (the 1960s) when both the student body and the curriculum were becoming more diverse.

Frye proved more efficient in removing partisan politics and hermeneutic doubt by claiming a special coherence for the field of literary studies. The concern inherited from the Romantics, and pre-eminently from Blake, about the rise and fall of vision, was adapted to an inventive though still teachable nomenclature. Frye's work suggested that the visionary energy associated with democratic ideals was dying, and that only the use of public education to revive the arts—arts that belonged to everyone, to humankind irrespective of social class or location—could realize the Arnoldian ideal of culture or the even older ideal of a republic of letters.

I see more good in past practices than some of you may be willing to concede. It is illogical, in terms of our mission, to displace the literary from the center of attention, and to allow ethics or politics to swallow just about everything. It is not easy, of course, to define the literary without essentializing. I do not have a *belles lettres* conception in mind but a quality of attention derived from the study of poetry and fiction and the more inventive kinds of expository or philosophical prose. The more I learn about English as a university subject, and modernity as an era in which it developed, the more I appreciate the tremendous play of forces that make the study of literature—and literature itself perhaps—a vulnerable endowment. "English must be kept up." When Keats wrote those words he was thinking about . . . O, many things: the glory and burden of Milton; the mother-tongue, or how a native tradition might be strengthened amid classical and sublime influences; and how to answer the greeting of a beautiful September morning by employing nature's own means, its undidactic language of the heart.

We can't keep literary study going without a combination of learning, enthusiasm, and—a bit of preaching, natural or unnatural. Yet the New Social Didacticism should recall that preaching and art are uneasy partners. Poetics has always placed the specificity of literature, or as Horace wittily said, its point (*punctum*), in moderating such pointing by mixing sweet and useful. Virginia Woolf can hardly be accused of disengagement from the world, but her attitude toward preaching is totally that of Horace or Keats. Reading in 1932 an edition of D.H. Lawrence's letters, she remarks characteristically though unfairly:

To me Lawrence is airless, confined. . . . I don't want "a philosophy" in the least. . . . What I enjoy . . . is the sudden visualisation: the great ghost springing over the wave . . . but I get no satisfaction from his explanations of what he sees. . . . Then too I dont like strumming with two fingers—& the arrogance. After all English has one million words: why confine yourself to 6? & praise yourself for so doing. But its the preaching that rasps me. . . . Art is being rid of all preaching: things in themselves: the sentence in itself beautiful. . . .[13]

When our social conscience acts up, which is much of the time, then there is a temptation to attack art in the name of a more realistic, demystified language. My retrospective suggests that this is unnecessarily self-mortifying. It also suggests that we should cease to underestimate the one "institution" vernacular literary studies have developed from sources reaching back to Montaigne, and whose "familiar" bent rethinks rather than rejects both technical terms and new realisms.

The essay, which is a *mentalité* not only a literary convention, has always been a genre within literature rather than an outsider. The essay is not one thing, of course, but a brief baggy monster; yet there is a consistency to it. From the outset it has been reflective rather than doctrinal, taking the reader as an equal, and conducting itself as a good-humored and provisional report. It does not contain startling news except in mock-heroic moments that parody its journalistic rival. (The animosity between journalist and literary critic, so obvious in the present culture wars, is that of enemy brothers.) Irremediably occasional, the essay tries to channel rather than suppress or inflame time-bound observations that keep flooding in, from the world or the self-haunting mind. While clearly issuing from a situated intellectual or scholar, the essay questions, as Emerson would say, its own instruments: whether these are the values it proposes or the very rhetoric by which they are affirmed. That makes its relation to doxa, public opinion, or the believable a complicated matter; and there are those who consider the essayistic form as too playful. But the danger is rather that the essay should succumb to a jargon of civility. Still, during the interwar years, both liabilities—excess of irony, excess of civility, sometimes even in combination—become more crucial: they provide a counterbalance to an oracular style of cultural prophecy, to a contagiously Nietzschean portentousness. I quote from the opening of Nietzsche's *The Will to Power*, a book that continues to move me but is symptomatic of this problem of style:

What I relate is the history of the next two centuries. I describe what is coming, what can no longer come differently. . . . The future speaks even now in a hundred signs. . . . Our whole European culture has been moving as toward a catastrophe, with a tortured tension that is growing from decade to decade: restlessly, violently, headlong, like a river that wants to reach the end, that no longer reflects, that is afraid to reflect.

More provocative than Nietzsche's fatalism[14] is the style. Some fifty years earlier, in *Sartor Resartus*, Carlyle had created a pseudo-Germanic ("Teufelsdröckhian") challenge to English complacencies. Nietzsche turns Carlyle's half-pedantic, half-prophetic manner against Germany itself—a Germany that has defeated France and is a nation-state sitting dangerously in the middle of Europe. His "Signs of the Times" prophetism amplifies a temptation which the essay as a genre resists. The essay maintains a *prosaic* alertness, a post-prophetic mode of thinking and writing. But reality has conspired with Nietzsche, and now an age of atrocity makes it more difficult to avoid this apocalyptic tone. "It's a wild time in the Near West, between one revelation and another," Wyndham Lewis wrote after a war that encompassed all of Europe.[15] That Wild Near West is still our habitat.

NOTES

1. Jean Baudrillard, *La transparence du mal: essai sur les phénomènes extrêmes* (Paris: Galilée, 1991).

2. William James, *Pragmatism*, Lecture 8.

3. This issue has often been raised in terms of the "class" to which intellectuals belong. Are they, consciously or not, members of a socio-economic class? Or is their value, precisely, that they belong to an "inter-class stratum," as Karl Mannheim thought and Sartre restates when he describes them as "perpetually unclassed," because of their inside-outside status? "The

intellectual's duty is to live his contradiction *for all* and to surpass it *for all* by his radicalization (in other words, by the application of techniques of truth to lies and illusions). Precisely because of his contradiction, he tends to become a guardian of democracy." "What Is an Intellectual?," in *Between Existentialism and Marxism: Sartre on Philosophy, Politics, Psychology and the Arts,* trans. John Mathews (New York: Pantheon, 1974). Originally in *Situations VIII* (Paris: Gallimard, 1972).

4. For example, up to the end of World War II it was often suggested that the exclusion of Jews from English departments was not racially motivated but based on the fact that English literature, and European culture generally, were Christian.

5. I realize that, according to some, philosophy or science too may retain an ideological element.

6. See Paul de Man, *The Resistance to Theory* (Minneapolis: University of Minnesota Press, 1986), especially the title essay.

7. *The Resistance to Theory,* p. 26.

8. Correlatively, an unresolved tension arises between method and truth. While the pedagogical can flourish on the plane of method, and many theorists of the purer kind were superb teachers, on the plane of truth the pedagogical is displaced by the didactic, which is quite a different sort of passion.

9. See Franz Rosenzweig, *Briefe,* ed. Edith Rosenzweig (Berlin: Schocken Verlag, 1935), p. 653. "Der *anthropos theoretikos* [Greek lettering in the original], diese grösste und dauerhafteste, weil in ihr selbst ohne Antithesis gebliebene (selbst die Ideen haben doch in der Antike selbst schon ihr Nein gefunden) Zeugung der Griechen, hat eben endgültig cessé de regner." A translation of the letter can be found in Eugen Rosenstock-Huessy, ed., *Judaism Despite Christianity* (University, Alabama: University of Alabama Press, 1969), pp. 91–92. Emmanuel Levinas quotes Rosenzweig in *Difficile liberté: Essais sur le judaisme* (Paris: Albin Michel, 1963, rpt. 1976), p. 241. Cf. Levinas, *Totality and Infinity,* trans. Alphonso Lingis (Pittsburgh: Duquesne University Press, 1969), pp. 42–48. For Martin Buber, see *I and Thou* (1923). The most influential source for "anti-self-consciousness" is Carlyle's essay "Characteristics" (1831), which was known to Nietzsche. My thanks to Jill Robbins for help in tracking down the quotations.

10. We should be preoccupied, Leavis declared, "not with the generalizations of philosophical and moral theory and doctrine, but with picking up a continuity; carrying on and fostering the essential life of a time-honored and powerful institution, in this concrete, historical England": *Education and the University* London: Leavis thus resisted the idea of an English Tripos paper on the novel in general rather than on the English novel. Proust and Kafka were a misdirection, he claimed. "The coherent course would be the English novel from Dickens to Lawrence." (See Raymond Williams, in Denys Thompson, ed., *The Leavises: Recollections and Impressions* [Chatto & Windus, 1943. New York: Cambridge University Press, 1984]).

11. Leavis was more absolute in excluding both science and philosophy: he cut through questions of interpretive principle by "fingering" texts as if they were touchstones, by using his tactical gift to move from passage to passage until his judgment seemed validated without extraneous argument. Staying that close to literary sources, and refusing—most of the time—to extravert a motivating and ultimately irrelevant mystique, he too contributed powerfully to the new "practical" criticism.

12. "On the Teaching of Modern Literature," in *Beyond Culture* (New York: The Viking Press, 1968).

13. *The Diary of Virginia Woolf,* ed. Anne Oliver Bell (New York and London: Harcourt Brace Jovanovich), IV (1982), p. 126.

14. The river metaphor, in the above quotation, is as much a call to immerse in the destructive element as a dire warning that we must stop and reflect. The lover in Lamartine's "Le Fleuve" asks the river (time) to suspend its flow, but this "lover of fate" is closer to the rhetorical music of a *Liebestod.*

15. *Time and the Western World* (1928).

4.

The Welcome Table

HENRY LOUIS GATES, JR.

Let's set the stage. Take one young, eager, black American journalist—that was me. One aging actress/singer/star—that was Josephine Baker. And one luminary of black letters: James Baldwin. I was 22, a London-based correspondent for *Time* magazine, and I felt like a mortal invited to dine at his personal Mount Olympus.

My story, for which the magazine had agreed to fund my trip to France, was on "The Black Expatriate." One of my principal subjects was Baldwin. Another was Josephine Baker who, being a scenarist to her very heart, put a condition on her meeting with me. I was to arrange her reunion with Baldwin, whom she hadn't seen since she left France many years ago to live in Monte Carlo.

Well into her 60s in 1973, Josephine Baker still had a lean dancer's body. One expected that. She was planning a return to the stage, after all. What was most surprising was her skin, smooth and soft as a child's. The French had called her "cafe-au-lait," but that says nothing of the translucency or the delicate shading of her face. Her makeup was limited to those kohl-rimmed eyes, elaborately lined and lashed, as if for the stage. She flirted continually with those eyes, telling her stories with almost as many facial expressions as words.

I do not know what she made of me, with my gold-rimmed cool-blue shades and my bodacious Afro, but I was received like a dignitary of a foreign land who might just be a long-lost son. And so we set off, in my rented Ford, bearing precious cargo from Monte Carlo to Saint Paul-de-Vence, Provence, *chez* Baldwin. In case I was in any danger of forgetting that a living legend was my passenger, her fans mobbed our car at regular intervals. Invariably, she responded with elaborate grace, partly playing the star who expects to be adored, partly the aging performer who was simply grateful to be recognized.

Baldwin made his home just outside the tiny ancient walled town of St. Paul-de-Vence, nestled in the alpine foothills that rise from the Mediterranean Sea. The air carries the smells of wild thyme, pine, and centuries-old olive trees. The light of the region, prized by painters and vacationers, at once intensifies and subdues colors, so that the terra-cotta tile roofs of the buildings are by turns rosy pink, rust brown, or deep red.

His house—situated among shoulder-high rosemary hedges, grape arbors, acres of peach and almond orchards, and fields of wild asparagus and strawberries—was built in the eighteenth century and retained its original frescoed walls and rough-hewn beams. And yet he had made of it, somehow, his own Greenwich Village café. Always there were guests, a changing entourage of friends and hangers-on. Always there was drinking and conviviality. "I am *not* in paradise," he assured readers of the *Black Scholar* that year, 1973. "It rains down here too." Maybe it did. But it seemed like paradise to me. And if the august company of Jo Baker and James Baldwin wasn't enough, Cecil Brown was a guest at St. Paul, too: Cecil Brown, author of the campus cult classic, *The Life and Loves of Mister Jiveass Nigger,* and widely esteemed as one of the great black hopes of contemporary fiction.

The grape arbors sheltered tables, and it was under one such grape arbor, at one of the long harvest tables, that we dined. Perhaps there was no ambrosia, but several bottles of Cantenac Braun provided quite an adequate substitute. The line from the old gospel song, a line Baldwin had quoted toward the end of his then-latest novel, inevitably suggested itself: *"I'm going to feast at the welcome table."* And we did, we did.

I wondered why these famous expatriates had not communicated in so long, since St. Paul was not far from Monte Carlo. I wondered what the evening would reveal about them, and I wondered what my role in this drama would be. It was the first time Jo and Jimmy had seen each other in years; it would prove the last.

At that long welcome table under the arbor, the wine flowed, food was served and taken away, and James Baldwin and Josephine Baker traded stories, gossiped about everyone they knew and many people they didn't, and remembered their lives. They had both been hurt and disillusioned by the United States and had chosen to live in France. They never forgot, or forgave. At the table that long, warm night, they recollected the events that led to their decisions to leave their country of birth, and the consequences of those decisions: the difficulty of living away from home and family, of always feeling apart in their chosen homes; the pleasure of choosing a new life, the possibilities of the untried. A sense of nostalgia pervaded the evening; for all their misgivings, they shared a sense, curiously, of being on the winning side of history.

And with nostalgia, anticipation. Both were preparing for a comeback. Baker would return to the stage in a month or so; and it was on stage that she would die. Baldwin, whose career had begun so brilliantly, was now struggling to regain his voice. The best was yet to come, we were given to understand.

People said Baldwin was ugly; he himself said so. But he was not ugly to me. There are, of course, faces that we cannot see simply as faces because they are so familiar that they have become icons to us, and Jimmy's visage was one such. And as I sat there, in a growing haze of awe and alcohol, studying his lined face, I realized that neither the Jimmy I had met—mischievous, alert, and impishly funny—nor even the Jimmy I might come to know, could ever mean as much to me as James Baldwin, my own personal oracle, that gimlet-eyed figure who had stared at me out of a fuzzy dust jacket photograph when I was fourteen. For that was when I met Baldwin first and discovered that black people, too, wrote books. You see, that was *my* Baldwin. And it was strictly Private Property. No trespassing allowed.

I was attending an Episcopal church camp in eastern West Virginia, high in the Allegheny Mountains overlooking the South Branch of the Potomac River. It was August 1965, a month shy of my fifteenth birthday. This, I should say at the outset, was no ordinary church camp. Our themes that year were "Is God Dead?" and "Can you love two people at once?" (*Dr. Zhivago* was big that summer, and Episcopalians were never ones to let grass grow under their feet.) After a solid week of complete isolation, a delivery man, bringing milk and bread to the camp, told the head counselor that "all hell had broken loose in Los Angeles," and that the "colored people had gone crazy." Then he handed him a Sunday paper, screaming the news that Negroes were rioting in some place called Watts.

I, for one, was bewildered. I didn't understand what a riot was. Were colored people being killed by white people, or were they killing white people? Watching myself being watched by all of the white campers—there were only three black kids among hundreds of campers—I experienced that strange combination of power and powerlessness that you feel when the actions of another black person affect your own life, simply because you both are black. For I knew that the actions of people I did not know had become my responsibility as surely as if the black folk in Watts had been my relatives in the village of Piedmont, just twenty or so miles away.

Sensing my mixture of pride and discomfiture, an Episcopal priest from New England handed me a book later that day. From the cover, the wide-spaced eyes of a black man transfixed me. *Notes of a Native Son,* the book was called, by one James Baldwin. Was this man the *author,* I wondered to myself, this man with a closely cropped "natural," brown skin, splayed nostrils, and wide lips, so very Negro, so comfortable to be so?

It was the first time I had heard a voice capturing the terrible exhilaration and anxiety of being a person of African descent in this country. From the book's first few sentences, I was caught up thoroughly in the sensibility of another person—a black person. The book performed for me the Adamic function of naming the complex racial dynamic of the American cultural imagination. Coming from a tiny, segregated black community in a white village, I knew both that "black culture" had a texture, a logic, of its own *and* that it was inextricable from "white" culture. That was the paradox that Baldwin identified and negotiated, and that is why I say his prose shaped my identity as an Afro-American, as much by the questions he raised as by the answers he provided. If blackness was a labyrinth, Baldwin would be my cicerone, my Virgil, my guide. I could not put the book down.

I raced through this book, then others, filling my commonplace book with his marvelously long sentences, bristling with commas and qualifications. Of course, the biblical cadences spoke to me with a special immediacy. For I, too, was to be a minister, having been "saved" in a small black evangelical church at the age of twelve. (From this fate as well, the Episcopalians—and, yes, James Baldwin—diverted me.) I devoured his books: first *Notes,* then *Nobody Knows My Name, The Fire Next Time,* and then *Another Country.* I began to imitate his style of writing, using dependent clauses whenever and wherever I could—much to my English teacher's chagrin. Consider:

And a really cohesive society, one of the attributes, perhaps, of what is taken to be a "healthy" culture, has, generally, and I suspect, necessarily, a much lower level of tolerance for the maverick, the dissenter, the man who steals the fire, than have societies in which, the common ground of belief having all but vanished, each man, in awful and brutal isolation, is for himself, to flower or to perish.

(Nobody Knows My Name)

There are 16 commas in that sentence; in my essays at school I was busy trying to cram as many commas into my sentences as I could—until Mrs. Iverson, my high school English teacher, forbade me to use them "unless absolutely necessary!"

Poring over his essays, I found that the oddest passages stirred my imagination. There were, for example, those moments of the most un-

Negro knowingness, a cosmopolitanism that moved me to awe: such as his observation that, unlike Americans,

Europeans have lived with the idea of status for a long time. A man can be as proud of being a good waiter as of being a good actor, and in neither case feel threatened. And this means that the actor and the waiter can have a freer and more genuinely friendly relationship in Europe that they are likely to have here. The waiter does not feel, with obscure resentment, that the actor has "made it," and the actor is not tormented by the fear that he may find himself, tomorrow, once again a waiter.

I remember the confident authority with which I explained this insight (uncredited, I suspect) about French and American waiters to a schoolmate. It hardly mattered that there were no waiters in Piedmont, W.V., unless you counted the Westvaco Club, which catered to the management of our one industry, a paper mill. It mattered less that there were no actors. How far was Paris, really? Baldwin wrote about an epiphany experienced before the cathedral in Chartres. In Piedmont, true enough, we had no such imposing monuments, but I struggled to collect his noble sentiments as I stood before our small wooden church, in need though it was of a fresh coat of white paint.

   I, of course, was not alone in my enthrallment and, much as it vexed me, Baldwin was *not* my private property. When James Baldwin wrote *The Fire Next Time* in 1963, he was exalted as *the* voice of black America. The success of *Fire* led directly to a cover story in *Time* in May of 1963; soon he was spoken of as a contender for the Nobel Prize. ("Opportunity and duty are sometimes born together," Baldwin wrote later.) Perhaps not since Frederick Douglass a century earlier had one man been taken to embody the voice of "the Negro." By the early sixties, his authority seemed nearly unchallengeable. What did the Negro want? Ask James Baldwin.

   The puzzle was—as anyone who read him should have recognized—that his arguments, richly nuanced and self-consciously ambivalent, were far too complex to serve straightforwardly political ends. Thus he would argue in *Notes of a Native Son* that

the question of color, especially in this country, operates to hide the graver question of the self. That is precisely why what we like to call "the Negro problem" is so tenacious in American life, and so dangerous. But my own experience proves to me that the connection between American whites and blacks is far deeper and more passionate than any of us like to think. . . . The questions which one asks oneself begin, at last, to illuminate the world, and become one's key to the experience of others. One can only face in others what one can face in oneself. On this confrontation depends the measure of our wisdom and compassion. This energy is all that one finds in the rubble of vanished civilizations, and the only hope for ours.

One reads a passage like this one with a certain double-take. By proclaiming that the color question conceals the graver questions of the self, Baldwin leads us to expect a transcendence of the contingencies of race, in the name of a deeper artistic or psychological truth. Instead, with an abrupt swerve, Baldwin returns us to them.

In America, the color of my skin had stood between myself and me; in Europe, that barrier was down. Nothing is more desirable than to be released from an affliction, but nothing is more frightening than to be divested of a crutch. It turned out that the question of who I was was not solved because I had removed myself from the social forces which menaced me— anyway, these forces had become interior, and I had dragged them across the ocean with me. The question of who I was had at last become a personal question, and the answer was to be found in me.

I think that there is always something frightening about this realization. I know it frightened me.

Again, these words are easily misread. The day had passed when a serious novelist could, as had Thomas Mann at thirty-seven, compose his *Betrachtungen eines Unpolitischen*. Baldwin proposes not that politics is merely a projection of private neuroses, but that our private neuroses are shaped by quite public ones. The retreat to subjectivity, the "graver questions of the self," would lead not to an escape from the "racial drama," but—and this was the alarming prospect Baldwin wanted to announce—a rediscovery of it. That traditional liberal dream of a nonracial self, unconstrained by epidermal contingencies, was hopefully entertained and, for him at least, reluctantly dismissed. "There are," he observed,

few things on earth more attractive than the idea of the unspeakable liberty which is allowed the unredeemed. When, beneath the black mask, a human being begins to make himself felt one cannot escape a certain awful wonder as to what kind of human being it is. What one's imagination makes of other people is dictated, of course, by the laws of one's own personality and it is one of the ironies of black-white relations that, by means of what the white man imagines the black man to be, the black man is enabled to know who the white man is.

This is not a call for "racial understanding": on the contrary, we understood each other all too well, for we have invented one another, derived our identities from the ghostly projections of our alter egos. If Baldwin had a central political argument, then, it was that the destinies of black America and white were profoundly and irreversibly intertwined. Each created the other, each defined itself in relation to the other, and each could destroy the other.

For Baldwin, then, America's "interracial drama" had "not only created a new black man, it has created a new white man, too." In that sense, he could argue, "the history of the American Negro problem is not merely shameful, it is also something of an achievement. For even when the worst has been said, it must also be added that the perpetual challenge posed by this problem was always, somehow, perpetually met."

These were not words to speed along a cause. They did not mesh with the rhetoric of self-affirmation that liberation movements require. Yet couldn't his sense of the vagaries of identity serve the ends of a still broader, braver politics?

As an intellectual, Baldwin was at his best when exploring his own equivocal sympathies and clashing allegiances. He was here to "bear witness," he insisted, not to be spokesman. And he was right to insist on the distinction. But who had time for such niceties? The spokesman role was assigned him willy-nilly.

The result was to complicate further his curious position as an Afro-American intellectual. On the populist Left, the then-favored model of the oppositional spokesman was what Gramsci called the "organic intellectual": someone who participated in and was part of the community he would uplift. And yet Baldwin's basic conception of himself was formed by the familiar, and still well-entrenched, idea of the alienated artist or intellectual, whose advanced sensibility entailed his estrangement from the very people he would represent. Baldwin could dramatize the tension between these two models—he would do so in his fiction—but he was never to resolve it.

A spokesman must have a firm grasp on his role, and an unambiguous message to articulate. Baldwin had neither, and when this was discovered a few short years later, he was relieved of his duties, shunted aside as an elder, and retired, statesman. The irony is that he may never fully have recovered from this demotion from a status he had always disavowed.

And if I had any doubts about that demotion, I was set straight by my editor at *Time* once I returned to London. They were not pleased by my choice of principal subjects. Josephine Baker, I was told, was a period-piece, a quaint memory of the twenties and thirties. And as for Baldwin: well, wasn't he passé now? Hadn't he been for several years?

Baldwin, *passé?* In fact, the editor, holding a wet finger to the wind, was absolutely correct, and on some level I knew it. If Baldwin had once served as a shadow delegate for black America in the congress of culture, his term had expired. Besides, soldiers, not delegates, were what was wanted these days. "Pulling rank," Eldridge Cleaver wrote in his essay on Baldwin, "is a very dangerous business, especially when the troops have mutinied and the basis of one's authority, or rank, is devoid of that interdictive power and has become suspect."

Baldwin, who once defined the cutting edge, was now a favorite target for the *new* cutting edge. Anyone who was aware of the ferment in black America was familiar with the attacks. And nothing ages a young Turk faster than still younger Turks.

Baldwin was "Joan of Arc of the cocktail party," according to the new star of the black arts movement, Amira Baraka. His "spavined whine and plea" was "sickening beyond belief." He was—according to a youthful Ishmael Reed—"a hustler who comes on like Job."

Eldridge Cleaver, the Black Panther's Minister of Information, found in Baldwin's work "the most gruelling agonizing, total hatred of the blacks, particularly of himself, and the most shameful, fanatical, fawning syco-phantic love of the whites that one can find in any black American writer of note in our time." Above all, Baldwin's sexuality represented treason: "Many Negro homosexuals, acquiescing in this racial death-wish, are out-raged because in their sickness they are unable to have a baby by a white man." Baldwin was thus engaged in "a despicable underground guerilla war, waged on paper, against black masculinity." Young militants referred to him, unsmilingly, as Martin Luther Queen.

Baldwin was, of course, hardly a stranger to the sexual battlefield. "On every street corner," Baldwin would later recall of his early days in Green-wich Village, "I was called a faggot." What was different this time was a newly sexualized black nationalism that could stigmatize homosexuality as a capitulation to alien white norms, and correspondingly accredit homo-phobia—a powerful means of policing the sexual arena—as a progressive political act.

A new generation, so it seemed, was determined to define itself by everything Baldwin was *not*. By the late sixties, Baldwin-bashing was almost a rite of initiation. And yet Baldwin would not return fire, at least not in public. He responded with a pose of wounded passivity. If a new and newly militant generation sought to abandon him, Baldwin would not abandon them.

In the end, the shift of political climate forced Baldwin to simplify his rhetoric or else risk internal exile. As his old admirers saw it, Baldwin was now chasing, with unseemly alacrity, after a new vanguard, one that es-teemed rage, not compassion, as our noblest emotion. "It is not necessary for a black man to hate a white man, or to have particular feelings about him at all, in order to realize that he must kill him," he wrote in *No Name in the Street,* a book he started writing in 1967 but did not publish until 1972. "Yes, we have come, or are coming, to this, and there is no point in flinching before the prospect of this exceedingly cool species of fratricide

. . . ." That year he told the *New York Times* of his belated realization that "our destinies are in our hands, black hands, and no one else's." A stirring if commonplace sentiment, this, which an earlier Baldwin would have been the first to see through.

How far we had come from the author of *The Fire Next Time,* who had forecast the rise of black power and yet was certain that "we, the black and the white, deeply need each other here if we are really to become a nation—if we are really, that is, to achieve our identity, our maturity, as men and women. To create one nation has proved to be a hideously difficult task; there is certainly no need now to create two, one black, and one white." All such qualms were irrelevant now. In an off-handed but calculated manner, Baldwin affected to dismiss his earlier positions: "I was, in some way, in those years, without entirely realizing it, the Great Black Hope of the Great White Father." Now he knew better.

In an impossible gambit, the author of *No Name in the Street* sought to reclaim his lost authority by signaling his willingness to be instructed by those who had inherited it: this was Baldwin and the new power generation. He borrowed the populist slogans of the day and returned them with a Baldwinian polish. "The powerless, by definition, can never be 'racists,' " he writes, "for they can never make the world pay for what they feel or fear except by the suicidal endeavor that makes them fanatics or revolutionaries, or both; whereas those in power can be urbane and charming and invite you to those which they know you will never own." The sentiment in its unadorned rendering—that blacks cannot be racist—is now a familiar one, and often dismissed as an absurdity; but the key phrase here is "by definition." For this is not a new factual claim, but a rhetorical move. The term "racism" is redefined to refer to systemic power relations, a social order in which one race is subordinated to another. (A parallel move is common in much feminist theory, where "patriarchy"—naming a social order to which Man and Woman have a fixed and opposed relation—contrasts with "sexism," which characterizes the particular acts of particular people.) It cannot, therefore, be dismissed as a factual error. And it does formulate a widely accepted truth: the asymmetries of power mean that not all racial insult is equal. (Not even a Florida jury is much concerned when a black captive calls his arresting officer a "cracker.")

Nonetheless, it is a grave political error: for black America needs allies more than it needs absolution. And the slogan—a definition masquerading as an insight—would all too quickly serve as blanket amnesty for our dankest suspicions and bigotries. It is a slogan Baldwin once would have repudiated, not for the sake of white America—for them, he would have argued, the display of black prejudice could only provide a reassuring confirmation of their own—but for the sake of black America. The Baldwin who knew that the fates of black and white America were one knew that if racism was to be deplored, it was to be deplored *tout court,* and without exemption clauses for the oppressed. Wasn't it this conviction, above all, that explained his repudiation of Malcolm X?

I should be clear. Baldwin's reverence for Malcolm was real, but posthumous. In a conversation with the psychologist Kenneth Clarke, recorded a year and a half before the assassination, Baldwin ventured that by preaching black supremacy, "what [Malcolm] does is destroy a truth and invent a myth." Compared to King's appeal, Malcolm's was "much more sinister because it is much more effective. It is much more effective, because it is, after all, comparatively easy to invest a population with false morale by giving them a false sense of superiority, and it will always break down in a crisis. That is the history of Europe simply—it's one of the reasons that we are in this terrible place." But, he cautioned, the country "shouldn't be worried about the Muslim movement, that's not the problem. The problem is to eliminate the conditions which breed the Muslim movement." (Five years later, under contract with Columbia Pictures, Baldwin began the task of adapting Malcolm to the silver screen.)

That ethnic scapegoating was an unaffordable luxury had been another of Baldwin's lessons to us. "Georgia has the Negro," he once pithily wrote, slicing through thickets of rationalization, "and Harlem has the Jew." We have seen where the failure of this vision has led: the well-nigh surreal spectacle of urban activists who would rather picket Korean grocery stores than crack houses, presumably on the assumption that sullen shopkeepers with their pricey tomatoes—not smiley drug dealers and their discount glass vials—are the true threat to black dignity.

The sad truth is that as the sixties wore on, Baldwin, for all his efforts, would never be allowed to reclaim the cultural authority he once enjoyed. To give credit where credit is due, the media can usually tell the difference between a trend-maker and a trend-follower. What did the Negro *really* want? Ask Eldridge Cleaver.

I did. Several months after my visit to St. Paul-de-Vence, I returned to France to interview the exiled revolutionary. We had moved with the times from cosmopolitan expatriates to international fugitives. ("How do I know you're not a CIA agent?," he had demanded when we first talked.) This was not a soirée on the Riviera. It was an apartment on the Left Bank, where Eldridge and Kathleen lived, and where he put me up in his study for a couple of weeks; here, ostensibly, was the radical edge that Baldwin now affected to covet.

Between Cleaver and Baldwin, naturally, no love was lost. Eldridge complained to me that Baldwin was circulating a story about him impugning his manhood. He wanted me to know it was untrue. He also wanted me to know that he would soon be returning and would take up where he had left off. The talk was heady, navigating the dialectical turns of Fanon and Marx and Mao and Ché. (Jesus would be added a few months later.) His shelves were lined with all the revolutionary classics, but also W.E.B. Du Bois, Richard Wright, and, yes, James Baldwin. Young Baldwin may have warned of "the fire next time," but Cleaver, determined to learn from the failures of his revolutionary forebears, was busily designing the incendiary devices.

What came as a gradual revelation to me was that Cleaver really wanted to be a writer, and that Baldwin was, perforce, his blueprint of what a black writer could be. He was at work, he told me, on a memoir, to be entitled *Over My Shoulder;* on a novel, to be called *Ahmad's Jacket.* But commitment, to be genuine, had to spill over the page. And in case I forgot our parlous position in the nether-zone of the law, there was that hijacker—armed, dangerous, and definitely deranged—who had insisted on staying with them, too. Eldridge, who had adopted me as a younger brother for the nonce, handed me a butcher's knife to keep under my pillow and made sure I propped a filing cabinet in front of the door before I went to sleep at night.

Times had changed all right. That, I suppose, was our problem. But Jimmy wanted to change with them, and that was his.

We lost his skepticism, his critical independence. Baldwin's belated public response to Cleaver's charges was all too symptomatic. Now, with slightly disingenuous forbearance, he would turn the other cheek and insist, in *No Name in the Street,* that he actually admired Cleaver's book. Cleaver's attack on him was explained away as a regrettable if naïve misunderstanding: the revolutionary had simply been misled by Baldwin's public reputation. Beyond that, he wrote,

I also felt that I was confused in his mind with the unutterable debasement of the male—with all those faggots, punks, and sissies, the sight and sound of whom, in prison, must have made him vomit more than once. Well, I certainly hope I know more about myself, and the intention of my work than that, but I *am* an odd quantity. So is Eldridge, so are we all. It is a pity that we won't, probably, ever have the time to attempt to define once more the relationship of the odd and disreputable artist to the odd and disreputable revolutionary. . . . And I think we need each other, and have much to learn from each other, and, more than ever, now.

It was an exercise in perversely *willed* magnanimity, meant, no doubt, to assure us that he was with the program; and to suggest, by its serenity, unruffled strength. Instead, it read as weakness, the ill-disguised appeasement of a creature whose day had come and gone.

Did he know what was happening to him? His essays give no clue, but then they wouldn't. Increasingly, they came to represent his official voice, the carefully crafted expression of the public intellectual, James Baldwin. His fiction became the refuge of his growing self-doubts.

In 1968, he published *Tell Me How Long the Train's Been Gone*. Formally speaking, it was his least successful work. But in its protagonist, Leo Proudhammer, Baldwin created a perfectly Baldwinian alter-ego, a celebrated black artist who, in diction that matched that of Baldwin's essays, could express the quandaries that came increasingly to trouble his creator. "The day came," he reflects at one point, "when I wished to break my silence and found that I could not speak: the actor could no longer be distinguished from his role." Thus did Baldwin, our elder statesman, who knew better than anyone how a mask could deform the face beneath, chafe beneath his own.

Called to speak before a civil rights rally, Proudhammer ruminates upon the contradictions of his position. "I did not want others to endure my estrangement, that was why I was on the platform; yet was it not, at the least, paradoxical that it was only my estrangement which had placed me there? . . . [I]t was our privilege, to say nothing of our hope, to attempt to make the world a human dwellingplace for us all; and yet—yet—was it not possible that the mighty gentlemen, my honorable and invaluable confreres, by being unable to imagine such a journey as my own, were leaving something of the utmost importance out of their aspirations?"

These are not unpolitical reflections, but they are not the reflections of a politician. Contrast Leroi Jones's unflappable conviction, in an essay published in 1963: "A writer must have a point of view, or he cannot be a good writer. He must be standing somewhere in the world, or else he is not one of *us*, and his commentary then is of little value." It was a carefully aimed arrow and it would pierce Baldwin's heart.

The threat of being deemed "not one of *us*" is a fearful thing. *Tell Me How Long* depicts a black artist's growing sense that (in a recurrent phrase) he no longer belongs to himself. That his public role may have depleted the rest of him. There is a constituency he must honor, a cause he must respect; and when others protect him, it is not for who he is, but what he stands for.

To be sure, what Baldwin once termed "the burden of representation" is a common malady in Afro-American literature; but few have measured its costs—the price of that ticket to ride—as trenchantly as he. Baldwin risked the fate that Leo Proudhammer most feared: which was to be "a Jeremiah without convictions." Desperate to be "one of us," to be loved by us, Baldwin allowed himself to mouth a script that was not his own. The connoisseur of complexity tried to become an ideologue. And with the roaring void left by the murders of Malcolm X and Martin Luther King, he must have felt the obligation ever more strongly.

However erratic some of his later writing might have been, I believe he could still do anything he wanted with the English essay. The problem was, he no longer knew what he wanted . . . or even what we wanted from him. Meanwhile, a generation had arrived that didn't want anything from him—except, perhaps, that he lay down and die. And this, too, has been a consistent dynamic of race and representation in Afro-America. If someone has anointed a black intellectual, rest assured that others are busily constructing his tumbrel.

In an essay he published in 1980, he reflected on his role as an elder statesman: "It is of the utmost importance, for example, that I, the elder, do not allow myself to be put on the defensive. The young, no matter how loud they get, have no real desire to humiliate their elders and, if and when they succeed in doing so, are lonely, crushed, and miserable, as only the young can be." The passage is eloquent, admirable . . . and utterly, utterly unpersuasive.

We stayed in touch, on and off, through the intervening years, often dining at the Ginger Man when he was in New York. Sometimes he would introduce me to his current lover, or speak of his upcoming projects. But I did not return to St. Paul-de-Vence until shortly after his death three years ago, when my wife and I came to meet Jimmy's brother, David.

St. Paul had changed remarkably in the twenty or so years since he settled there. The demand for vacation homes and rental property has claimed much of the farmland that once supported the city and supplied its needs. Luxury homes dot the landscape on quarter-acre plots, and in the midst of this congestion stood Baldwin's ten-acre oasis, the only undivided farm acreage left in St. Paul. Only, now the grape arbors are strung with electric lights.

There we had a reunion with Bernard Hassell, Jimmy's loving friend of so many decades, and met Lucien Happersberger, the friend to whom *Giovanni's Room* is dedicated. After a week of drinking and reminiscing, David Baldwin asked me just when I had met Jimmy for the first time. As I recounted the events of our visit in 1973, David's wide eyes grew wider. He rose from the table, went downstairs into Jimmy's study—where a wall of works by and about Henry James faces you as you enter—and emerged with a manuscript in hand. "This is for you," he said.

He handed me a play, the last work Jimmy completed as he suffered through his final illness, entitled "The Welcome Table." It was set in the Riviera, at a house much like his own, and among the principal characters were "Edith, an actress-singer/star: Creole, from New Orleans," "Daniel, ex-black Panther, fledgling play-wright" with more than a passing resemblance to Cecil Brown, and "Peter Davis, Black American journalist." Peter Davis—who has come to interview a famous star, and whose prodding questions lead to the play's revelations—was, I should say, a far better and more aggressive interviewer than I was, but of course Baldwin, being Baldwin, had transmuted the occasion into a searching drama of revelation and crisis. Reading it made me think of all the questions I had left unasked. It was and is a vain regret. Jimmy loved to talk and he loved language, but his answers only left me with more questions.

Narratives of decline have the appeal of simplicity, but Baldwin's career will not fit that mold. "Unless a writer is extremely old when he dies, in which case he has probably become a neglected institution, his death must always seem untimely," Baldwin wrote in 1961, giving us fair warning. "This is because a real writer is always shifting and changing and searching." Reading his late essays, I see him embarking on a period of intellectual resurgence. I think he was finding his course, exploring the instability of all the categories that divide us. As he wrote in "Here Be Monsters," an essay published two years before his death, and with which he chose to conclude *The Price of the Ticket,* his collected nonfiction: "each of us, helplessly and forever, contains the other—male in female, female in male, white in black, and black in white. We are a part of each other. Many of my countrymen appear to find this fact exceedingly inconvenient and even unfair, and so, very often, do I. But none of us can do anything about it." We needed to hear these words two decades ago. We need to hear them today.

Times change. Madonna, our very own zeitgeist goddess, has recently announced her interest in seeing a film made of *Giovanni's Room,* which was one of Baldwin's greatest hopes. (In the late seventies, Robert De Niro and Marlon Brando were said to be interested in the project, but nothing came of it.) An influential intellectual avant-garde in black Britain has resurrected him as a patron saint. And a new generation of readers has come to value just those qualities of ambivalence and equivocality, just that sense of the contingency of identity, that made him useless to the ideologues of liberation and anathema to so many black nationalists. But then, even his fiercest antagonists have now welcomed him back to the fold. Like everyone else, we like our heroes dead.

"I suspect, though I cannot prove it," Baldwin wrote a decade before his death, "that each life moves full circle—toward revelation." Once again, he leaves us with a question. For whose revelation did he have in mind: his, or ours?

5.

The Institutionalization of Feminist Criticism

JANE GALLOP

In an essay published in 1987 Barbara Christian asserts: "In no way is the literature Morrison, Marshall, or Walker create supported by the academic world. Nor given the political context of our society, do I expect that to change soon. For there is no reason, given who controls these institutions, for them to be anything other than threatened by these writers."[1] Two years earlier, in 1985, Hortense Spillers states: "The American academy, despite itself, is one of the enabling postulates of black women's literary community simply because it is not only a source of income for certain individual writers, but also a point of dissemination and inquiry for their work."[2]

Spillers would agree that those who control these institutions have every reason to be "threatened by these writers"; that is the purport of her "despite itself." But the radical claim that "in no way is this literature supported by the academic world" must come up against a few facts. For example: Toni Morrison has taught at Columbia, Yale, and Princeton Universities; Paule Marshall has a permanent position at Virginia Commonwealth University; Alice Walker has taught at Wellesley and held a Radcliffe Institute Fellowship (with an appointment by the Harvard Corporation). And then there are the courses which require the purchase of books by these women as well as disseminating awareness of their work. And beyond the classroom, a growing industry in academic articles and conference papers on these very writers.

Spillers continues: "The image of black women writing . . . is conduced toward radical revision. The room of one's own explodes its four walls to embrace the classroom, the library, and the various mechanisms of institutional . . . life, including conferences, the lecture platform . . . and collections of critical essays" (250). Delivered as a lecture at a woman's college by a non-academic, Virginia Woolf's *A Room of One's Own,* extremely mindful of the material and institutional infrastructures of knowledge and culture, offers the unforgettable image of the woman writer barred from the library. Recalling Woolf, Spillers points out that black women writing are no longer excluded from the library.

I have been quoting from Spillers's Afterword to *Conjuring,* the 1985 "collection of critical essays" on black women's fiction that she edited with Marjorie Pryse. The first time I read that collection, I was disappointed that the volume was so "academic." I disliked the references to Ovid, to *The Golden Bough,* to deism. When I found an essay particularly "academic," tracing similarities to classical mythology or simply too dry in style, I would imagine that *this* critic must be white. Since I am a white academic, what sort of fantasy not only renders those attributes contemptible but, from an imagined identification with some righteous outside, allows me to cast them as aspersions on others?

The 1985 Pryse and Spillers anthology conjures up the image of that powerful outside and then catches me in full fantasy to recall that these critics are writing and I am reading them within the white man's academy. Spillers's Afterword states: "Some of the fiction writers whose works are discussed here are (or were) also teachers in the academy, just as the critics are, so that the site of the institution becomes as crucial an aspect of the whole discussion as the audience toward which this volume of essays is aimed" (249).

My topic here is the institutionalization of feminist criticism; what, it might be asked, do I think about that? I think it is a fact. And I notice it is a fact rarely spoken of objectively. The word "institutionalization" sounds like some form of incarceration. The academicization of feminist criticism is generally discussed as if it had happened *against our will.*

Academic feminists accuse other academic feminists of being "academic." This sort of aggressive dissociation clouds our understanding of how we got here. None of us just woke up one day to discover that she had a Ph.D., a full-time academic job, much less tenure. This disavowal of the academic also deflects us from the question of what we ought to and could do now that we have a voice within this institution. We don't seem very able to theorize about how we speak, as feminists wanting social change, from *within* our positions in the academy.

Around 1981 American feminist literary criticism entered the heart of a contradiction. It became secure and prospered in the academy while feminism as a social movement was encountering major setbacks in a climate of new conservatism. The Reagan-Bush years began; the ERA was defeated.

In the American academy feminism gets more and more respect while in the larger society women cannot call themselves feminist.

My insistence that we recognize that we are, or that feminist criticism is, in the academy has sometimes been taken for a celebration of that fact. I worry that my statements will be sucked into a machine which demands that one either condemn "academic feminism" or stand accused as an "academic feminist." If I'm not bemoaning the selling out of feminist criticism to academic respectability, then I must be one of those bourgeois feminists whose only goal is such respectability. Maybe I am; one shouldn't be too quick to deny any accusation voiced by more than the odd individual. But I continue to feel the necessity for an analysis which includes the academic location of the accusers.

I do not want to celebrate our being in. Being in something that is a transmitter of elitist values. Being in a discourse that is constituted, at this point in time, as marginal to the larger culture and society. But I do not want to bemoan it either. I want to understand why we are located here, how we got here, what we sacrificed to get here, what we gained: all as preliminaries to the question of how do we do the most good, as feminists, as social and cultural critics, speaking from this location.

Much talk about institutionalization implicitly construes institutions as monolithic, unchanging, or even inherently evil. Institutions have histories, are in history. When we conceive of them as unchanging, we have less chance of wittingly affecting their direction. "Institutionalization," writes Meaghan Morris, "is not another name for doom, that fate always worse than death. It's an opportunity, and in many instances a necessary condition, for serious politics."[3]

The institution here is the literary academy, which is at once a discursive field, a pedagogical apparatus, a place of employment, a site of cultural reproduction, an agency of cultural regulation, and an institution generally marginal to power and values in American society. What *we* can most effectively say and do as feminists is mediated through this institution, its ideologies, values, structures, and its location in the world.

Within the literary academy, the term "criticism" refers to what, by the 1960s, was certainly the most commonly practiced form of scholarship: textual interpretation. Outside of literary studies, "literary criticism" is more likely to mean some form of evaluation (the book review) and "criticism" unmodified has the primarily negative sense of fault-finding. Feminists writing about literature described our practice as "criticism" in order, I believe, to take advantage of the double sense of the word. It could imply, when necessary, that we were engaged in a negative evaluation, a "critique," of a cultural institution; it could also signify, when appropriate, that we were simply doing what students of literature did. This double sense worked well for a group located on the margins of an institution, expressing our position as at once critical of and obedient to the discipline.

In 1984 *Tulsa Studies in Women's Literature* published a double issue entitled "Feminist Issues in Literary Scholarship." In this title, the word "scholarship" replaces the ambiguous "criticism." These are "Feminist Issues," but they are "Feminist Issues *in* Literary Scholarship." In that 1984 *Tulsa Studies* Jane Marcus cites an earlier essay by the journal's editor: "Shari Benstock suggests . . . that academic feminist critics are not marginal in the least, compared to black outsiders or writers excluded from the academy."[4]

In 1983 Benstock takes over from Germaine Greer the leadership of a journal devoted to the study of women's literature. Her first editorial refers to "those of *us* inside the circle (academics who practice feminist literary criticism)"[5] and also calls for contributions to the 1984 special issue. Her editorial preface to that 1984 special issue, subtitled "A Letter from Paris," circles around the confrontation between feminist criticism and French poststructuralism.

Two major trends shaped American academic feminist criticism in the late 1970s: (1) Feminist criticism was implicitly defined as studies in women's literature and (2) French-style poststructuralist feminism appeared in this country. Both trends, I believe, contributed enormously to the acceptance of feminist criticism by the literary academy. The first helped define feminist criticism as a subfield, thus giving it a place within literary studies without necessarily calling the whole into question, as well as making it seem like every English department should have one. The second rode in on the coattails of the quick rise of deconstruction in American English Studies. "Theory" included a "feminist" component, although it also dismissed feminist criticism that was not properly "theoretical." These two trends have usually been opposed in feminist critical histories, but I would contend that they not only were strikingly contemporaneous but that, as separate and distinct strategies for feminist inclusion, they worked, if unwittingly, together. By the mid-eighties readings of women's literature based in poststructuralist theory are very widespread and constitute the center of academic feminist criticism.

In 1983 Benstock notes that feminists are academic insiders. In 1984 Marcus lists two sorts of writers more marginal than academic feminists: "black outsiders or writers excluded from the academy." I would say that a major gesture of academic feminist literary criticism in the late 1980s has been the inclusion of "black outsiders." White feminist critics by the dozens have turned to writing about black women writers. Finally, we started listening to what black feminists had been saying for over a decade (if not a century), although too often listening just long enough to rush out and quickly try to do the right thing. As I speak these words in 1991, we can envision an inclusion of black women writers in the literary academy paralleling the inclusion of white women writers in the 1980s. But Marcus's second category, "writers excluded from the academy," could pose a more troubling problem for us academic feminists, if we understand it not as those contingently excluded (the writers we fight to get into the canon) but as the structural, institutional exclusion of the non-academic, of those who might challenge our values, those who are excluded by the very processes which constitute our inclusion.

The literary academy takes as its central purpose the transmission of a culture superior to "popular" culture. Literary criticism has traditionally tried to determine what is superior and to help the general reader, the student, appreciate those higher things to be found in literature. A central piece of the ideology of the literary academy is the belief that the artist is not only a craftsman but wise, a superior human being. Where traditional criticism loves to show that the well-wrought verse or sentence or plot also contains fundamental humanist understandings, feminist criticism is enamored of the writer whose exquisite sentences can be shown to express whatever feminist theory the critic espouses. Behind this belief is the notion of an artistic elite, an aristocracy of talent, who not only write well, but are simply superior. Through the appreciation of great literature, which all of us who teach literature foster unless we actually contest it, we further the appreciation of great individuals.

When New Criticism held sway in the literary academy, the reigning values were aesthetic. By the mid-1980s the dominant discourse in the literary academy is poststructuralist and the reigning values are theoretical. Where once the academic feminist looked to Emily Dickinson, now she pins her hopes on Julia Kristeva. When feminist criticism devotes itself to geniuses like Dickinson and Kristeva, it contradicts feminism by preferring the woman who is different from and better than other women.

A decade ago feminist criticism was racked by debate over poststructuralist theory. In retrospect we can also see that as a debate about the institutionalization of feminist criticism. By the end of the eighties conflict over race has become the point of densest energy in academic feminism. This one is not a theoretical debate: no white critic claims we should ignore race or stick to writing about white women. But between feminists there is the same intensity, anxiety, and anger sparked by the earlier debate. Race was by and large not a question, for white literary academics, in the seventies. I would contend that one reason it is such a heated topic now is that it is also a displaced discussion of the institutional status of feminist criticism, an anxious non-encounter with the fact of our specific location as insiders.

The last half-decade has witnessed a massive turn to literature by other women, first and foremost African-Americans but then also, more recently, moving to other ethnic groups and other nationalities. This moment, which continues as I speak, already has to its credit two major accomplishments: the inclusion of questions of race in critical considerations of gender and the inclusion of writings by African-American women in academic practice—critical and pedagogical, feminist and mainstream—in particular, the works of Hurston, Morrison, and Walker.

These inclusions substantially alter both feminism and criticism. But, subject to these revitalizing corrections, what remains is still the study of literature by women. And although it does wondrous good to view black women as producers of the highly valued cultural product "literature," questions about the boundaries of the literary realm, about the possible elitism of the category itself, are deferred by the inclusion of these exemplary representatives of the doubly oppressed.

During the classic period of feminist literary criticism, from 1975 to 1983, the question of why study literature rarely was posed. By the late eighties, "literature" as object of feminist criticism no longer goes without saying. Feminist criticism has participated in a more general move from literary to cultural studies. Within cultural studies, literature is looked at as one among various signifying practices rather than as a privileged site of "culture."

This challenge calls into question the very grounds and ideology of the discipline. But it also must be said that feminist cultural criticism in the late 1980s is taking place in the context of a literary discipline that is interrogating itself and transmuting into cultural studies.

From the standpoint of this challenge to the elitism of high culture, the claims that Euro-American women or even African-American women can produce high culture might seem merely reformist. But it also must be remembered that, in an academy which takes itself and is taken by the larger society as a purveyor of a culture that is better, it is of significant effect to associate that highness, however we might also and at the same time want to call it into question, with representatives of inferiorized groups, for example women and people of color.

We may want to use our limited but real cultural authority, as purveyors of "better culture," teachers for example, both to link women to culture, wisdom, and knowledge in order to chip away at hierarchies which associate us with nature, body, the menial and yet also to use that same authority to call the ideology of high culture into question.

Between 1975 and 1983 the mainstream of academic feminist criticism implicitly defined its enterprise in a way that fit the literary academy. Cooptation or strategy? We may not be able simply to decide what motivated this fit. But we live in the legacy of that period; we benefit from

THE INSTITUTIONALISM OF FEMINIST CRITICISM

it. It allows us not only radically to call its terms—"women" and "literature"—into question but to be heard through an institution's channels of transmission when we do so.

From the point of view of contemporary trends, feminist literary criticism of the classic period looks irretrievably tame. But we must also see, looking retrospectively at that period, that, once installed, feminist criticism was precisely free to move in more radical directions and it immediately did so. Although we often are merciless about the blind spots of the 1975–1983 period, our contemporary challenges are in fact possible because of the solid institutional foothold gained through the tame definition of feminist criticism.

Now that we are comfortable enough to ask these questions and be heard, let us use this position not to accuse each other of being too academic or elitist or reformist but to articulate these questions with the institution in which we work and through which we interact with society, we feminists in what is still, until further notice, the literary academy.

NOTES

1. Barbara Christian, "The Race for Theory," first appeared in *Cultural Critique* 6 (Spring 1987), reprinted in Linda Kauffman, ed., *Gender and Theory: Dialogues on Feminist Criticism* (Oxford: Basil Blackwell, 1989), p. 235.

2. Hortense J. Spillers, "Afterword: Cross-Currents, Discontinuities: Black Women's Fiction," in Hortense J. Spillers and Marjorie Pryse, eds., *Conjuring: Black Women, Fiction, and Literary Tradition* (Bloomington: Indiana University Press, 1985), p. 249.

3. Meaghan Morris, "*in any event* . . .," in Alice Jardine and Paul Smith, eds., *Men in Feminism* (New York: Methuen, 1987), p. 179.

4. Jane Marcus, "Still Practice, A/Wrested Alphabet: Toward a Feminist Aesthetic," first appeared in *Tulsa Studies in Women's Literature* 3, 1–2 (1984), reprinted in Shari Benstock, ed., *Feminist Issues in Literary Scholarship* (Bloomington: Indiana University Press, 1987), p. 87.

5. Shari Benstock, "The Feminist Critique: Mastering Our Monstrosity," *Tulsa Studies in Women's Literature*, 2 (Fall 1983): 141, emphasis added.

6.

Sodometries

JONATHAN GOLDBERG

In November, 1990, just a few months after the Iraqi invasion of Kuwait, and in the midst of U.S. preparations for war, an ad for a Tee shirt appeared in *Rolling Stone*. "Americans, Make a Statement," the ad read; below it was displayed the image that "Americans" might sport: a U.S. flag appears in the background, partially obscured by a camel; superimposed on the camel's rump—obligingly turned to meet the viewer's gaze—is the face of the Iraqi leader, smiling, slightly open-mouthed, his head swathed in Arab headdress. What statement were "Americans" to make? A sentence surrounds the picture; it reads: "America Will Not Be Saddam-ized."[1] The statement equates Saddam Hussein's invasion of Kuwait with rape, and implies that all forced entries are acts of sodomy. Saddam Hussein is, thereby, represented as homosexual, as the highly stigmatizing depiction makes clear. Saddam's head is where the camel's tail would be; hence, the face, quintessentially human, is, in this image, animal; Hussein's mouth replaces the camel's asshole, and the reversal of front and back also implies an equation of anal and oral sex. Homosexuality, thus linked to bestiality and to indiscriminate, promiscuous sexual behavior, is further tainted by all the ways in which the face reads as foreign—heavy black holes for eyes and mouth, black lines for eyebrows and moustache; racial difference is insistent, while the headdress—not usually worn by Hussein—is feminizing. Although Saddam Hussein is declared to be a sodomizer, the homophobia that fuels the picture aggressively sodomizes him.

Appearing in *Rolling Stone,* this ad could be regarded as aimed at a particular audience—presumably, a youthful rockcult one. Yet the appeal of such an image hardly can be confined to a rock 'n' roll crowd of whatever age, nor relegated to a particular segment of the population. Moreover, the work that the ad does is not only a manifestation of popular culture or dismissable as such. For the image trades in a militaristic *imaginaire,* one that frighteningly has seemed all too available in the past year, as anyone who listened to the military briefings that saturated the media during the U.S. war with Iraq can testify. The Tee shirt is part of the war effort licensed by Congress and the White House. Nonetheless it would be a mistake, I think, to regard such saturation as complete or as entirely successful. Even the Tee shirt logo and image, however complicit they might be with the recruitment of *Rolling Stone* readers for the campaign of military mobilization, is also knowing, almost witty. Indeed, the shirt says something that otherwise remained buried, virtually unspeakable and unacknowledged on

the airwaves and in most newspapers, happy, it appeared, to report the news as the military supplied it: the shirt declares the complicities of racism, sexism, and homophobia mobilized by the war. A certain amount of demystification is performed by the image; it might even be thought to empower its wearer with a degree of knowledge.

For the statement made by this Tee shirt is not an entirely straightforward one. Perhaps only to my Renaissance-trained eyes, the shirt seems amenable to a reading that might recognize in its image repertoire not only the complex overdeterminations of the present moment—confluences and conflicts within and between popular culture, the media, late-capitalist commodification, the military, the government—but also certain strange historic overlaps. Structured as the image is by confusions of before and behind, head and tail, flag and camel, the statement it makes seems to me if not "utterly confused," to borrow Foucault's characterization of sodomy before the advent of modernity and the modern regimes of sexuality, at the very least confused with those supposedly archaic registers.[2] As in the "ancient civil or canonical codes" to which Foucault alludes in the introductory volume of his *History of Sexuality* (43), sodomy is equated with bestiality, as it is in the first English sodomy law, passed during the reign of Henry VIII, which punishes with death those convicted of "the detestable and abhomynable vice of buggery commyttid with mankynde or beaste";[3] as in that formulation, the sexual act lacks specificity—it might be oral or anal sex, performed by "mankind" or with an animal. Insofar as Saddam is feminized—or, indeed, insofar as Kuwait is thought of as a woman taken from behind—crossings of gender, so-called unnatural sex, in the favored language of Blackstone for instance, even the trope of inversion that serves as one major definition of homosexuality from the nineteenth century on, also are implicated in the image. Fantasies that equate homosexuality with molestation are involved. Sodomy as the vice of Mediterranean/Islamic cultures, a recurring notion in English Renaissance texts, still seems available too.

If the image traffics in these highly sedimented registers that go back over several historical periods, all more or less out of date one might have supposed, the representation is organized by a classical trope, *histeron proteron*, anglicized by George Puttenham, the Elizabethan Kenneth Burke,[4] as the preposterous. Puttenham defines the trope as a form of disordered speech in which the cart is put before the horse; *histeron proteron* borders on the tropes that Puttenham finds "notoriously undecent" (182); yet the preposterous, he opines, is "tolerable enough, and many times scarce perceivable" (181).[5] Part of the work this image does can be understood in these terms: it borders on obscenity, yet locates indecency in what Saddam Hussein has done, not what the image does. Interestingly, among Puttenham's examples of the preposterous is a line of poetry in which the speaker first claims a kiss and then departs. Puttenham worries about whether that order is backwards or not and decides finally that on this question, "yong Courtiers" (181) can decide. The preposterous is thus a trope involving questions of sexual decorum; although reversing before and behind could mean crossing over the boundary that separates licit from illicit behavior, it might as easily be a question managed by those who do it all the time, and have the capacity to make such transgressions seem utterly ordinary. These confusions—and normalizations—of before and after also may guide our reading of the historical sedimentation of the image. If this shirt says, we will not be sodomized, it also demystifies what must be done in order not to be in that supposedly passive position. For the ad does not simply invite "Americans" to make a statement, it calls for action. If the American flag has been desecrated, covered and recovered by the images of camel and Saddam's face, a reversal of the image is called for by the image's own reversals. What are "Americans" to do? Aim at the bullseye, the target on the camel's rear; clear the space so that the flag will be uncovered. "We will not be Saddam-ized"; the flag that is unfurled behind will come before, as a missile of penetration. Within the tropologics of this reversible statement, if we say that "we will not be sodomized," our actions will reverse that deplorable condition. In a word, "America" says, "we will sodomize."

Saddam—homosexual, bestial, foreign, inhuman, feminine—is the target of a proper masculinity: America's degradation is nothing less than its being placed behind, its passivity (feminine, homosexual) in a sexual act the image asks its viewers to reverse. In the layout of the shirt, the word "America" appears above the image, the rest of the sentence below it. Momentarily, it might appear as if the word "America" titled the image. To read the image that way would be to produce, in Puttenham's terms, an indecency, an image of America that includes the foreign, the homosexual, the woman, an America, in a word, that has subscribed to cultural pluralism; all this follows from the equation of Kuwait and America upon which the image depends and which it also disavows. Rather, to read the image and statement properly—which is to say, backwards—we must produce something that will not seem reversed at all. Imperceptibly, as Puttenham suggested, the image can be made tolerable enough so doing, and the complicities upon which it trades can be effaced. Even as "America" is invited to perform an act—Saddam's act—that act must be read and done otherwise. But the image only knows front and behind, and it trades in the equation of oppositions. Unavoidably, the image asks us to be sodomites, a message delivered quite explicitly by another Tee shirt in support of the war; it depicts a missile and bears the logo: "Hey Saddam This Scuds [sic] For You!!"; the missile's target is Saddam's rearend.[6] If Saddam is blasted away, if the homosexual is destroyed, it would be impossible ever to suppose that proper male aggression could be misrecognized as sodomy. First, these images misrecognize Saddam's aggression as sodomy, then they claim the rights of aggression.

Looking at these images, we're not merely engaging in the vagaries of the signifier—Saddam's name is an accident that makes it available for a colonial *imaginaire* that could proceed without his name—nor are we simply dealing with the ever crossable and heavily policed border between the homosexual and the homosocial, the terrain of homophobia and homosexual panic. These representations raise some further questions: What place is sodomy assumed to have in the mind of the "America" being addressed? What is the purpose in these contemporary images of a sexual order whose confusions Foucault assigned to historic regimes before the advent of sexuality, indeed to a past that would seem to have been replaced by the regimes of modernity?[7] How and where does "that utterly confused category" survive and what work does it continue to do? Perhaps these are questions likely to occur only to someone who works "in" the Renaissance, but, I would argue, an inquiry into the ancient codes cannot be sealed off in some antiquarian preserve. Indeed, the invocation of historic difference— even the differences between the sodomite as "nothing more than the juridical subject" of forbidden acts and the homosexual as "a personage" (43) that Foucault so persuasively and magisterially laid out—cannot be used as a way of cordoning off the past from the present. The productive value of sodomy, even today, should not be underestimated. We need only recall the 1986 U.S. Supreme Court decision in *Bowers v. Hardwick* (106 S.Ct. 2841), with its declaration that the constitution of the U.S. recognizes no fundamental right of privacy for consensual acts of what the court termed homosexual sodomy, to see that the attitudes in these images are officially sanctioned ones. I turn to that decision now for the clearest evidence that the confusions of before and behind in which the image trades represent historic confusions capable of lethal mobilization.

A *University of Miami Law Review* piece,[8] cited by Justice Byron White in his majority opinion in *Bowers v. Hardwick* (2844), contemplates, in its concluding pages, the effects the decision of the court might have. First, opining that to uphold Georgia's sodomy statute would have no effect whatsoever—since states could continue to criminalize sodomy or not—the essay proceeds to the "major impact on both constitutional doctrine and on our society's view of homosexuals" that overturning the law would have. "A decision extending the right of privacy to homosexual activities could legitimize the gay rights movement," the essay concludes; "a contrary decision might reinforce negative attitudes toward homosexuals" (638). Within two pages, the affirmation that the "consequences of denying homosexual activities the protection of the right to privacy would be few" (636) leads to the recognition, faced, it would seem, with utter equanimity, that such a decision would license and endorse homophobia. Justice White

never acknowledges that effect as a consequence of his merciless decision—
he, too, claims that the decision leaves states free to pass the laws it chooses
and thus declares that the opinion of the majority "raises no question about
the right or propriety of state legislative decisions to repeal their laws that
criminalize homosexual sodomy, or of state-court decisions invalidating
those laws on state constitutional grounds" (2843). Rather than noting
that he knows what he is doing—promoting and encouraging homophobia,
White only acknowledges the *Miami Law Review* article as a source for its
historical survey of sodomy laws. It is under the cover of what passes for
history that White evades—and insures—the consequences that he pretends
the court's decision was not meant to unleash.

Drawing on previous decisions that define the fundamental rights guaranteed by the constitution as those " 'implicit in the concept of ordered
liberty' such that 'neither liberty nor justice would exist if [they] were
sacrificed,' " and as " 'deeply rooted in this Nation's history and tradition,' " White wrote: "it is obvious to us that neither of these formulations
would extend a fundamental right to homosexuals to engage in acts of
consensual sodomy. Prescriptions against that conduct have ancient roots"
(2844). White refers at this point to a page of the *Miami Law Review*
essay that declares that "current state laws prohibiting homosexual intercourse are ancient in origin" (525), and which offers as examples Plato's
Laws, the Sodom and Gomorrah story, a sentence from Leviticus, the
burning of "homosexuals as heretics" in the Middle Ages, and the English
statute of 1533 cited earlier. Governing this presentation of history is a
slippage from sodomy to homosexuality that occurs in the course of a single
sentence. The historical review opens, "At common law, and at one time
by statute in every state of the United States, sodomy was a criminal act"
(523). Next sentence: "Traditionally, states have considered homosexuality
to be 'sinful, sick, and criminal' " (524).

Several commentators have pointed out the superficiality of this history,
its fundamental errors in equating sodomy with homosexuality, as well as
factual errors in Justice White's next historical pronouncement, that "Sodomy was a criminal offense at common law and was forbidden by the
laws of the original thirteen states when they ratified the Bill of Rights.
In 1868, when the Fourteenth Amendment was ratified, all but 5 of the
37 States in the Union had criminal sodomy laws" (2844–2845).[9] Not
only are White's numbers suspect, but the content of sodomy laws changed
in the course of the years; what is effaced in this history is that ancient
sodomy laws *and the Georgia statute under consideration* do not distinguish
between hetero- and homosexual sodomy, that it is only in twentieth-
century legal formulations that oral sex—the crime that Michael Hardwick
was caught performing in his own bedroom—explicitly is included in the
definition of sodomy—in the nineteenth century, it explicitly was not.[10] The

Supreme Court decision tacitly upheld the right of heterosexuals to perform sodomitical sex and denied that right to homosexuals. Yet, it also defined homosexuals as those who perform that act, and several post-*Hardwick* decisions have affirmed that homosexuals now are by definition a criminal class.[11]

Those who have written about the historical errors in White's decision have taken it to task for its highly prejudicial account; much the same is the case for his source, and it is, it hardly needs saying, amazing to find Plato's *Laws* invoked as the touchstone for ancient Greek attitudes towards sex between men; by referring to the Sodom and Gomorrah story as a "legendary account," the *Miami Law Review* piece (525), it might be added, is more circumspect than White, or than Justice Warren Berger, whose concurring opinion invokes "millennia of moral teaching," and includes an approving citation of Blackstone's description of sodomy as " 'the infamous *crime against nature*' as an offense of 'deeper malignancy' than rape, a heinous act 'the very mention of which is a disgrace to human nature,' and 'a crime not fit to be named' " (2847). But more to the point here is a consideration of what has happened when sodomy, that utterly confused category, one of whose confusions lies precisely in failing to distinguish non-procreative homo- and heterosexual intercourse, is invoked in *Hardwick,* but now to secure the very difference between homo- and heterosexuality. Here it's worth remarking, as the dissenting justices did, that the Georgia statute in question in *Bowers v. Hardwick* was hardly an ancient one at all, having been enacted only in 1968, replacing at that time a sodomy law aimed solely at homosexual sex. That earlier law had proved to be too specific, had been found, for instance, not to obtain when two lesbians were brought to trial.[12] It is possible that the law was extended to include heterosexuals for fear that the earlier law might be challenged as unconstitutionally prejudicial; perhaps the only way to insure that the law could cover all possible cases lay in not specifying sexual orientation. For, it has to be added that however written, Georgia's laws, like those of other states, when enforced, have been used for the most part against presumptively gay men and lesbians. But it was recognized that that practice could only be shielded—indeed would only be possible—if the law pretended equality. The Supreme Court decision vacates the need for that pretense.

Between the codes of the colonies and the states of the union in 1861 and modern statutes, a change had occurred, the one that Foucault's argument details: from the sodomite, the juridical subject defined as anyone performing a sexual act not aimed at procreation within the bonds of marriage, to the homosexual as a particular form of identity. The 1968 change in Georgia's law tallies with the statutes on the books in the twenty-four states that continue to criminalize sodomy (only seven states restrict their sodomy laws to homosexuals). These laws, at least as written, do not discriminate overtly between identities. Acts are criminalized, not identities. Laws that would seem *textually* to evidence a continuity with the ancient statutes are *contextually* quite different however. Earlier sodomy laws were directed solely at acts because it was presumed that anyone might do them; homo- or heterosexual identity was not in question. Nonetheless those who have attempted to make the historic argument that the ancient statutes have nothing to do with the present have erred, not in insisting that sodomy and homosexuality are different, but in assuming that because sodomy comes from an older regime it no longer has a function. Paradoxical as it is, the decision of the Supreme Court, distinguishing homo- and hetero-sexual sodomy, follows from the modern regimes in which homo- and heterosexual identities are presumptively distinct. That presumption about identities allows the same act to read entirely differently when performed by persons who are assumed to embody these identities. The Foucauldian insistence that the sodomite is not the homosexual ignores not only the persistence of the sodomite as a means of defining homosexuality, but also how unstable the modern regime of supposedly discrete identities is. For when the Supreme Court attempts to define an identity through an act that it also permits to those whose identities are not defined by the per-formance of the same act, it leaves open the question of where heterosexual identity resides beyond the affirmation of a difference that has no content, an identity in other words that is defined by no specificity of acts but only by claims to be an identity.

These questions touch on the definitional impasse that Eve Kosofsky Sedgwick explores in *Epistemology of the Closet,* the difference between minoritizing definitions of homosexuality (which, she notes, have often been the basis for legal claims—e.g. to the rights due to a despised minority), and universalizing claims—those that declare that sexual identities take place across a continuum that artificially divides one sexual preference from another. The latter, as she suggests, might well be associated with the ancient regimes of the sodomite insofar as sodomy was assumed to be a temptation anyone might succumb to, rather than a marker of identity.[13] In this light the illegitimacy of the Supreme Court decision lay in its use of the equation of sodomy and homosexuality to attempt to separate the homo- and heterosexual on the basis of sodomy; the fault, that is, lay in the assumption about the relation of acts to persons, in the presumption of unbridgeable difference. It's that presumption that also underwrites the opinion of the dissenting justices, couched as it is in the language of liberalism, of individual rights and the right to privacy. As one law review essay has suggested, to protect homosexuality through arguments about the right to privacy offers no safeguards for homosexuality as a social identity—it assumes that homosexuals are defined solely by private sexual acts;[14] hence, as Robert Caserio has commented, both majority and minority views in the *Hardwick* decision agree that if homosexuals have any place at all it is the closet.[15] (The majority would have that closet barred and padlocked, of course.) Both views would keep homosexuality and homosexuals invisible. Public space is presumptively heterosexual; hence the Americans addressed by the Tee shirt with which we began can engage in acts of sodomy—even acts of homosexual sodomy—on the presumption that such acts do not define heterosexuals. To base rights for homosexuals on minoritizing definitions or in the right of privacy allows for the belief, now made law in *Bowers v. Hardwick,* that homosexuals and heterosexuals are so immutably different that their acts could never be the same—even when they are. As in the ancient codes, sodomy continues to perform the work of categorical confusion that is necessary to maintain the state. The alternative to this, as Janet Halley has suggested, would be the recognition that the difference between homo- and heterosexuality is always being breached, that in furthering the regimes of the closet, the *Hardwick* decision attempts to secure sexual difference even as it insures mechanisms for homosexual invisibility—i.e. guarantees that some gay-identified persons will pass as straight and that some straight-identified persons may be taken as gay. Her argument in support of the extension of equal rights to a public space of gay identity lies in the recognition that one can never know what homosexuality is or who is a homosexual.[16]

Or a sodomite. It is a remarkable fact that in many of the states in which sodomy remains a crime, the language used is identical to that found in Renaissance or colonial American statutes (25 Henry VIII. c.6 cited verbatim, for example, in Massachusetts, Michigan, Mississippi, Oklahoma, Rhode Island, and South Carolina, and with small variations elsewhere);[17] a Maryland court just a few years ago ruled that its law against "unnatural or perverted practice" was perfectly correct, not in the least vague, because *we all know what it means* not to say more specifically what the crime not to be named among Christians is.[18] But do we? States worried that such language is too vague have tried to specify the acts; this means that in different states, sodomy is variously defined; most often it is any act involving the genitals of one person and the mouth or anus of another; in some states, the tongue is added; in two, the hand; Texas adds to these that the introduction of any foreign object into a sexual organ constitutes an act of sodomy. In Missouri, a man who placed his hands on the clothed crotch of a police officer was found guilty of sodomy. The laws and the ways they have been enforced revel in fantasies of sexual acts that are limited only by the imaginations of the legislators—all of whom, we are to presume (they depend on it), are straight. Certainly our Supreme Court justices are; hence, while they keep intoning the phrase "ancient roots" and can't let go of the word "fundamental," we couldn't possibly hear sodomy in their language.[19]

How is it then that these acts are protected when performed by heterosexuals? How are heterosexuals differentially defined if their performance of these acts does not make them sodomites? The answer, as repetitiously intoned in *Bowers v. Hardwick* as is anything in the decision, is the institution of the family. Justice White's denial of a constitutional right to perform homosexual sodomy was situated in his affirmation that there is "no connection between family, marriage, or procreation" and "homosexual activity" (2844) and his definition of what is "deeply rooted in this Nation's history and tradition" (2846) as virtually synonymous with the family. Like sodomy, however, the family also is an empty concept—without content—even as it is taken to be the content of prior decisions involving the right to privacy. This is stunningly revealed in the *Miami Law Review* piece that White cites; having laid the ground for the Supreme Court decision by showing that previous privacy decisions have always taken place in the context of cases involving the married or marriageable couple or the families that result from marriage, and by indicating how often those earlier decisions have gone out of their way to exclude gays from them, the *Miami Law Review* piece attempts, rather half-heartedly, to argue that such decisions need not be so straitened, that there could be room for consensual homosexual sex within a broadened definition of the family. For, as the writers note, the family could be redefined not in terms of legal ties but in terms of affective ones, in ways that would validate what presumably makes the family a valuable, virtually sacred, institution—monogamy, care, long-term commitment, etc. But, following this logic, the *Review* is forced to conclude that to extend the family by defining it in this way might well mean that any number of married couples would no longer be protected by previous rulings. "The definition of family need not depend upon the sexual practices of its members but by the presence or absence of the attributes enumerated above," the *Review* concludes a section attempting to reconcile the traditional family to the equally longstanding liberal tradition that protects the individual. "The relationship must meet *all* the essential attributes to qualify for protection," the article continues. "Even a heterosexual relationship that is promiscuous would not qualify. Thus, the protection is for certain types of intimate relationships, and not for homosexuality or heterosexuality per se" (592).

There is, in this conclusion, a certain air of desperation, as the writers attempt to find what defines the value of the so-called family. Clearly, this was not a path down which the justices were willing to tread. By not giving any content to the concept of the family, *Bowers v. Hardwick* affirms that married or marriageable couples can perform any sexual acts in their bedrooms with complete impunity. But this also reveals that the private domain is defined solely in its relation to a public identity and to the laws that allow marriage only for male-female couples. (This ramifies to the defense of the individual offered by the dissenting justices, and not only to the regime of the closet noted earlier, for the individual affirmed, especially by Justice Stevens, is pronomially and presumptively male; even as equal rights for homo- and heterosexuals are affirmed by him, the rights are allotted, it appears, only to men.) Clearly enough, such privacy is shielded from public scrutiny because only some persons are allowed to have public identities. In that light, it seems worth arguing that so-called rights of privacy are shams; the bedroom has been policed beforehand. Freedom to do what one wishes is allowed only to those whose sexual acts the state will or could legitimize through the institution of marriage.

The consequences of this view are manifold. As Sylvia Law has argued, *Bowers v. Hardwick* depends throughout on a patriarchal view of sexual relations one might have thought to have been overturned in part by the very decisions about the rights accorded the family that the court cites as precedents;[20] of course, the most important of these is *Roe v. Wade,* and in a brief but telling essay, Norman Vieira has shown how *Bowers v. Hardwick* systematically undermines the principles at stake in that decision.[21] As he sees it, *Bowers v. Hardwick* was a rehearsal for overturning *Roe v. Wade.* "Given the striking conflict between the *Hardwick* opinion and the rationale of *Roe,* it must be asked whether the real target of the *Hardwick* case was homosexual sodomy . . . or the right of privacy in general and the *Roe* decision in particular," he concludes (1186). Both Law and Vieira contend that gender regulation is at the heart of the decision, and they are certainly right. Their arguments suggest that, once again, the line between homosexual and heterosexual is breached, and the very attempt to cordon homosexuals off as a criminal category fetches its arguments from ways in which the court wishes to enforce not merely heterosexuality but heterosexism. Law claims, convincingly, that the decision implicates the subordination of women within patterns of male domination; "the censure of homosexuality cannot be animated merely by a condemnation of sexual behavior," she argues (as I have been too), since the court allows the same sexual acts to be performed by heterosexuals. "Instead," she concludes, "homosexuality is censured because it violates the prescriptions of gender role expectations" (196).

Law's formulation that the decision was not, in her words, "merely" about homosexuality, like Vieira's claim that the "real target" in *Hardwick* was *Roe v. Wade,* runs the risk of the effacement, the rendering invisible of homosexuality that Law acutely sees is an aim in *Bowers v. Hardwick.* While there is no denying the importance of suggesting that the decision was not solely about gay rights, the way that point is made in both of these arguments conveys the unfortunate suggestion that the decision was important only insofar as it bears upon the relations between men and women, or upon a woman's rights to the control of her body. Rather, it is crucial in working out the implications of *Bowers v. Hardwick* not to seek to hierarchize oppressions but rather to trace the overdeterminations and discontinuities in the decision. Law is clearly on the mark, for example, when she notes that the patriarchal family affirmed by the decision is presumptively white and middle class (232–233); the decision has racist implications and to begin to address them one would want to note that historically sodomy laws have been used against blacks and immigrants far more often than against native-born whites.[22] One would want to pursue, as others beside Law have, following remarks made by Justices Blackmun and Stevens in their dissenting opinions, the startling relation between miscegenation laws and sodomy laws; African-Americans and whites were legally given the right to marry each other only in 1967, and the refusal to allow members of the same sex to marry is the catch-22 that the Supreme Court depends upon when it separates the family from same-sex couples.[23]

When Law and Vieira depend upon the hierarchy in which the "real" significance of *Bowers v. Hardwick* involves male-female relations they relegate homosexuals to a minority position; this is a consequence of the liberal values both writers uphold. By collapsing questions of sexuality into the "more important" realms of gender, homosexuality is allowed salience insofar as it seems assimilable to heterosexuality, insofar as same-sex relations are taken to be no different from cross-sex ones, a liberal tenet espoused as well by the dissenting justices in *Bowers v. Hardwick*. Yet the consequence of this assimilationist view is to deny differences that sexuality makes, and it is, once more, to model homosexuality in inversion, in the assumption that in any sexual relation, one person plays the male part and the other female role whatever their actual genders might be. Granting that the family that White appealed to is as atavistic an institution as the sodomy invoked to secure differences between hetero- and homosexuals, one must also suspect the implicit family structure, however liberalized it is, in Law or Vieira.

Once again, one may be struck by how these arguments resonate against Foucault, this time recalling his distinction between the apparatuses of alliance and sexuality, the former his shorthand term for the regulatory regimes that surround marriage, kinship ties, and inheritance, and that define the boundary between licit and illicit sexual acts in the ancient codes. As Foucault frames his argument, alliance was what the ancient laws and codes were all about, and the confusion of sodomy with a host of illicit activities resulted from the ways in which the laws put married procreative sex on one side of the line, and everything else on the other. The proliferating deployment of sexuality from the eighteenth century on, as Foucault argues, focuses its attention everywhere but on the couple that is at the center of the older regimes, on a whole series of potential disruptions to the norm of married life. As Foucault puts it, a silence surrounds the couple—"it

tended to function as a norm, one that was stricter, perhaps, but quieter"
(38)—while sex speaks noisily everywhere else. While, as he argues, alliance
does not disappear, but gives the law to sexuality, sexuality eroticizes alliance. Remarkably, given the ties between alliance and the law—the link
affirmed by invocations of the family—*Bowers v. Hardwick* allows the family
to be the sole domain of sexuality. Ruling against the legitimacy of sexuality
elsewhere, the perverse implantation is reimplanted within the couple. The
silence that makes the family as undefinable as anything in the decision
allows it all forms of sexual perversity. The justices and the legislators dream
of a perversity that homosexual sodomites perform, and, believing such
acts go on only there, license the same acts where they do not dream they
occur. Where they really occur, and not only in the fantasies of these
supposedly straight men.

Oddly enough, then, we return with this point to a strange continuity
with the old supposedly outmoded regimes of alliance. For if the point
about the ancient laws was that they imagined that anyone might perform
illicit acts, the new regime, clinging to the family, believes it can be allowed
anything because it cannot imagine it doing what is allowed. Homosexuality, as Sedgwick has argued, is the modern locus of the secret; but the
secret is not simply sutured to those who identify as or are identified as
homosexuals. Homosexuality is also the secret inside of heterosexuality,
nowhere more blatantly so than in the non-recognitions that structure the
Hardwick decision. If many gay men and women would just as soon have
nothing to do with the family, and might agree with Justice White—
though without appreciating his brutality and nastiness when he declared
that any relation between the rights of family members and the rights of
homosexuals is, in his words, "facetious" (2846)—it is because the joke is
on the institution that so anxiously defends itself against its own bankruptcy,
and that has been doing so in this country at least from the time of its
first sodomy laws. Such, at any rate, can be argued following Jonathan
Ned Katz's and other historians' explanations of why the colonists were so
intent on formulating laws against sodomy. It was a way of insuring the
patriarchal family.[24] And it requires only a glance at Alan Bray's crucial
book, *Homosexuality in Renaissance England,* or his recent essay on friendship and sodomy in the sixteenth century, to see why.[25] For, as Bray argues,
the hierarchies of Elizabethan society were oiled with sexual exchanges
between men. Sodomy is not, as he sees it, so much a set of forbidden
acts as the performance of those undefined acts—or the accusation of their
performance—by those who threatened social stability, heretics, spies, tra-
itors, Catholics. Colonial American prosecutions were virtually confined to
members of the lower classes, to those whose actions seemed to threaten
the prerogatives of the patriarchs. To the alliances made through marriage,
which are central to the legal apparatuses that Foucault details—and which

remain central to them at the level of ideological production—there are, there were, these other privileged ties between men, not all of which were secured by the exchange of women or the normalizing function of marriage. Even the colonial family therefore is an ideological structure, inserting women to secure political relations between men, cloaking male-male sexual possibilities (those that accrue to men as they are granted access to each other within a public sphere) with the thin veneer of family life as the sole domain of sexual behavior. The regimes of modernity have only furthered these illusions, and homo- and heterosexuality have been the means of securing supposedly unbreachable differences. The ancient family is the ideological linchpin of these misrecognitions, the speakable nexus of human relations to which the law remains atavistically—and productively—sutured.

Appeals to history always are shaped by present interests, and the justices' equation of the family with American foundations is not merely a partial point of view, but one indebted in every respect to the work that alliance serves, giving the law to modern regimes of sexuality. What would the justices, so intent on foundations, make, one wonders, of a passage from a text that, at least to some members of the literary community, has priority of place in American literature and that stands arguably as the foundational text for the new nation and a national imaginary? "O sacred bond . . . How sweet and precious were the fruits that flowed from the same!," it begins; but the bonds celebrated, however much they are written within a metaphorics of procreative sex, are those between men. This is the most exultant moment in William Bradford's *Of Plymouth Plantation,* and it celebrates the "ancient members," as he calls them, the founding fathers of the new nation, celebrates them, and mourns their demise and their irreplaceable loss. "I have been happy, in my first times, to see, and with comfort to enjoy, the blessed fruits of this sweet communion," Bradford writes, "but it is now a part of my misery in old age, to find and feel the decay and want thereof."[26] What, for that matter, might the justices make of an exchange of letters between John Winthrop and Sir John Spinge (brought to my attention by Michael Warner), in which Winthrop addresses his friend this way: "I loved you truely before I could think that you took any notice of me: but now I embrace you and rest in your love: and delight to solace my first thoughts in these sweet affections of so deare a friend." Like Bradford, Winthrop mourns his absent friend, and speaks his desire for him: "were I now with you," he writes, "I should bedewe that sweet bosome with the tears of affection."[27]

What might the justices make of this? No doubt they would remind us that Bradford's text is famous for a chapter, towards its close, decrying the spread of sodomy in Plymouth; no doubt they would cite the passage in Winthrop about the abominations in Massachusetts Bay, the case of William Plaine, who had "committed sodomy with two persons in England," and had gone on in New England to corrupt "a greater part of the youth of Guilford by masturbations . . . above a hundred times," who, moreover, "did insinuate seeds of atheism."[28] Would the justices note that the language of affection and the language of abjection is curiously identical, seed to seed? Or that Bradford, writing to the Governor of Massachusetts Bay about the outbreak of sodomy in his community, or Governor Bellingham, responding to him, with like concerns, sign themselves, "your loving friend"?

This border, between friend and sodomite, between the most exalted and most abjected bonds between men, is one whose negotiations are not confined to the past. The decision in *Bowers v. Hardwick* attempts, incoherently, to claim and disclaim this treacherous territory. It is in no way a singular document, however, and I want to close now with another set of letters that suggests further what interests—of the justices—were served by their decision.

In the summer of 1990, the *National Review* printed a letter from Marvin Liebman, longtime participant in the conservative movement, to his equally longtime friend William Buckley.[29] "We've known each other for almost 35 years now," Liebman noted; "I am almost 67 years old. For more than half my lifetime I have been engaged in, and indeed helped to organize and maintain, the conservative and anti-Communist cause" (17), he wrote, making his friendship with Buckley—"you are my best friend," the letter opens by declaring (16)—coincident with his political engagement. Liebman's public declaration of this coincidence was not, however, the aim of his letter; it was rather to announce his homosexuality. The letter was a public coming out by a man haunted by what he characterizes as the increasing homophobia of his political allies. Liebman explained why being gay and being conservative were compatible: that he had not chosen to be gay: "It is how I was born; how God decreed that I should be" (17); that "the conservative view, based as it is on the inherent rights of the individual over the state, is the logical political home of gay men and women" (18). To this letter, Buckley replied, oozing pity at his friend's pain, but pointing as the justices did in *Bowers v. Hardwick* to "the Judaeo-Christian tradition" and to the contradictory demand that Liebman's letter voiced, that a tradition "which is aligned with, no less, one way of life, [should] become indifferent to another way of life." Even granting that God made Liebman the way he is, Buckley went on, that could not shake "convictions rooted . . . in theological and moral truths," in what "we deem to be normal, and healthy" (18). At best, Buckley promised that the *National Review* would not engage in "thoughtless gay-bashing" though he qualified this promise by licensing the *Review* to indulge in "humor" (18): "I qualify this [promise] only by acknowledging that humor (if wholesomely motivated) is as irresistible to us, as it is to you."

Liebman's coming-out letter is a performance of the closet, with repeated hints that what he is declaring publicly in his letter will not surprise Buckley in the least. Buckley's sanctimonious reply is equally such a performance, trading in what "is as irresistible to us, as it is to you." Licensed by theological truths, by his own wholesomeness, Buckley can announce, in terms more open than anything Liebman says to his friend: "My affection and respect for you are indelibly recorded here and there, in many ways, in many places" (18), and can end his letter by declaring, "you remain, always, my dear friend, and my brother in combat." Drawing on the irresistible path that brought them together in the "cause I joined, along with you, 35 years ago," as Liebman puts it, Buckley trades on their affection, their brotherhood, their comradeship. Calling his dear friend "unnatural" (18), immoral, and unhealthy, he can, exercising Christian "toleration and compassion," also call him brother. Calling him *that* he need never notice how such terms of so-called compassion cover his irresistible bond to his friend, how irresistibly he can count on Liebman to take his humor as *thoughtful* gay-bashing, backed as it is by the church: "ten years ago," Liebman notes, "you served as my godfather when I entered the Catholic Church" (17). Re-closeted, reconverted, Liebman is instructed in Buckley's quasi-paternal message to recognize how he may remain the friend and comrade, what he must do to retain his love. And also, to maintain that precious individuality that joins him to the cause by subsuming it within the brotherly cause. It is at this point—as individuality is subsumed within brotherhood—that Buckley's language touches on the arguments of the liberal justices, the dissenting voices in *Bowers v. Hardwick;* that is, it is at this point that the conservative denial of homosexuality and the liberal affirmation of individuality meet in their insistence on the maintenance of the closet.

But whose closet is it? What does this exchange between Buckley and Leibman testify to, if not a continuation, however different the terms and the historical situation may be, of the calculated non-recognitions that structure the exchanges of letters penned by Bradford or Winthrop *and* their persecution of sodomites? What do these letters, written "here and there, in many ways, in many places," do, if not to vehiculate the (non)-relation of an abjected sexuality and an exalted love between men? Liebman worries in his letter that "without the anti-Communist and anti-tax movements as sustaining elements" (18) the assaults that he notices in TV evangelism and in the attempts to squash the NEA may burgeon into a campaign against gays as the uniting bond of the Christian brotherhood. Buckley assures him otherwise, even as he suggests just how that campaign will continue. What neither of them knew as they wrote in July 1990 was that a month later, a new campaign would be launched and that it would be aimed at someone all too conveniently named Saddam.

NOTES

1. *Rolling Stone*, November 15, 1990. I am grateful to Karin Cope for clipping this ad (for a First N Tees product) for me.

2. Michel Foucault, *The History of Sexuality: An Introduction,* trans. Robert Hurley (New York: Pantheon Books, 1978), p. 101. Further citations appear in the text.

3. 25 Hen. VIII. c.6. The law was first passed in 1533; it was renewed in 1536, 1539, and 1541. It was repealed and then re-enacted under Edward VI; the 1548 version of the law (2 & 3 Edw. VI. c. 29) is less stringent in its punishment than Henry's act, since, unlike the original statute, it allows the property of the person condemned to death under the statute to be inherited by his heirs. Mary repealed the law upon ascending the throne in 1553; in 1563, Elizabeth reinstated it and under the original Henrician terms (5 Eliz. c. 17), claiming that "Sithens wch Repeale so hadde and made dyvers evyll disposed psons have been the more bolde to committe the said most horrible and detestable Vice of Buggerie." The death penalty for sodomy remained on the books until 1861, when it was abolished in the Offenses Against the Person Act (24 & 25 Vict. c. 100). For a history of English sodomy laws, see H. Montgomery Hyde, *The Other Love* (London: Heinemann, 1970), pp. 29–57; Jeffrey Weeks, *Coming Out* (London: Quartet Books, 1977), pp. 11–22; and Ed Cohen, "Legislating the Norm: From Sodomy to Gross Indecency," in *Displacing Homophobia,* ed. R. Butters, J. Clum, and M. Moon (Durham, N.C.: Duke University Press, 1989). For further particulars on sixteenth-century English law, see Bruce R. Smith, *Homosexual Desire in Shakespeare's England* (Chicago: University of Chicago Press, 1991), pp. 41–53.

4. I owe this characterization of Puttenham to Barbara Herrnstein Smith.

5. All citations from George Puttenham, *The Arte of English Poesie* (Kent: Kent State University Press, 1970).

6. The image is reproduced in Richard Goldstein, "Season of the Kitsch: Watching and Shopping the War," *Village Voice* (March 15, 1991), p. 30. The complicities between "Sadam" and "Sodom" might well underlie a phenomenon noted by several commentators, President Bush's inability to pronounce properly Saddam Hussein's name. Calvin Trillin speculates on that question in a piece that appeared in the Raleigh, North Carolina *News and Observer* (and I assume in many other newspapers that carry his column) on March 11, 1991, "Reading Bush's lips for the key to victory." Trillin observes that the day that the war was declared won, Bush suddenly found he could say the name correctly. While Trillin believes that this manipulation was purposeful (some derogatory slur involved in the mispronunciation), it never occurs to him that (not) saying sodomy was involved; despite all his attempts to uncover a strategy, sodomy remains unthinkable for Trillin, and thus his analysis remains within the complicities that the strategy depends upon, what Eve Kosofsky Sedgwick has termed the privilege of unknowing in an essay that bears that title in *Genders* 1 (1988): 102–24.

For an incisive discussion of relationships between the war against Iraq, Bush's mispronunciations, misogyny, homophobia, and demonization, see Michael Bronski, "The Rape of Kuwait," *Gay Community News* (January 28–February 3, 1991), pp. 9, 11. I'm grateful to Heather Findlay for sending me the clipping.

7. The questions raised here and the suppositions guiding my discussion are everywhere informed by Eve Kosofsky Sedgwick's *Epistemology of the Closet* (Berkeley: University of California Press, 1990), esp. pp. 44–48. The discussion of *Bowers v. Hardwick* also follows her remarks on pp. 6–7, 86.

8. "Survey on the Constitutional Right to Privacy In the Context of Homosexual Activity," *University of Miami Law Review* 40 (1986): 521–657. Further page citations appear in the text.

9. The fullest historical critique is offered by Anne B. Goldstein, "History, Homosexuality, and Political Values: Searching for the Hidden Determinants of *Bowers v. Hardwick,*" *Yale Law Journal* 97 (1988): 1073–1103, esp. pp. 1081–1089.

10. Goldstein makes the point eloquently in "History, Homosexuality, and Political Values," p. 1086. For a review of nineteenth-century judicial decisions in which fellatio explicitly was ruled not to be included under sodomy statutes, see Lawrence R. Murphy, "Defining the Crime Against Nature: Sodomy in the United States Appeals Courts, 1810–1940," *Journal of Homosexuality* 19 (1990): 49–66.

11. *Padula v. Webster,* 822 F.2d 97 (D.C. Cir. 1987) is one such case. For a comment on the chilling effect that similar recent decisions may have on attempts to argue for gay rights within Fourteenth Amendment guarantees of Equal Protection, see the *Harvard Law Review* volume, *Sexual Orientation and the Law* (Cambridge, Mass.: Harvard University Press, 1990), pp. 168–170.

12. Justice Blackmun points this out in his dissenting opinion; see 106 S. Ct. 2849 and n. 1 for the failure of the previous Georgia sodomy law to be upheld in a case involving lesbians. Justice Stevens also stresses the point in his dissenting opinion; see 106 S. Ct. 2857.

13. See Sedgwick, *Epistemology of the Closet,* pp. 40–44, 83–90.

14. See the Note, "The Constitutional Status of Sexual Orientation: Homosexuality as a Suspect Classification," *Harvard Law Review* 98 (1985): 1285–1309, esp. pp. 1288–1292.

15. See Robert L. Caserio, "Supreme Court Discourse vs. Homosexual Fiction," in *Displacing Homophobia,* pp. 262–264.

16. See Janet E. Halley, "The Politics of the Closet: Towards Equal Protection for Gay, Lesbian, and Bisexual Identity," *UCLA Law Review* 36 (1989): 915–976, which has guided my discussion throughout.

17. For the texts of the statutes, see the Appendix to "The Right of Privacy and Other Constitutional Challenges to Sodomy Statutes," *Toledo Law Review* 15 (1984): 868–875. This piece seems to have been influential for the minority opinion in *Bowers v. Hardwick.* It is, of course, the case that citation of early English statutes in current law does not exhaust the question of the archaic quality of these formulations; descriptions of sodomy as the crime against nature or as an "unnatural" act have medieval origins, as James A. Brundage notes in Appendix 3, "Survivals of Medieval Sex Law in the United States and the Western World," in his *Law, Sex, and Christian Society in Medieval Europe* (Chicago: University of Chicago Press, 1987), p. 612.

18. For further consideration of this decision, see Halley, "Politics of the Closet," pp. 954–955. In the confusions of definition that I pursue, I follow Halley's discussion on pp. 949 ff. For details about state laws, see Halley, p. 919 n. 14, and *Sexual Orientation and the Law,* pp. 9–10. On the presumptions about knowledge, see Sedgwick, *Epistemology of the Closet,* p. 45 and chap. 4 passim.

19. I owe this point to a 1989 MLA Convention presentation by Lee Edelman.

20. See Sylvia Law, "Homosexuality and the Social Meaning of Gender," *Wisconsin Law Review* (1988): 187–235. Further citations appear in the text.

21. See Norman Vieira, "*Hardwick* and the Right of Privacy," *University of Chicago Law Review* 55 (1988): 1181–1191. Further citations appear in the text.

22. For some telling statistics for 1880, see Jonathan Katz, *Gay American History* (New York: Thomas Y. Crowell, 1976), p. 36, which shows that of the sixty-three people in jail at that time on sodomy convictions, thirty-two were classified as "colored," while of the thirty-one whites, eleven were foreign born.

23. See Blackmun 2845, Stevens 2857, and Andrew Koppelman, "The Miscegenation Analogy: Sodomy Law as Sex Discrimination," *Yale Law Journal* 98 (1988): 145–164.

24. See Jonathan Ned Katz, *Gay/Lesbian Almanac* (New York: Harper and Row, 1983), pp. 31–65 and, following Katz, John D'Emilio and Estelle B. Freedman, *Intimate Matters: A History of Sexuality in America* (New York: Harper and Row, 1988), pp. 15–38.

25. Alan Bray, *Homosexuality in Renaissance England* (London: Gay Men's Press, 1982); "Homosexuality and the Signs of Male Friendship in Elizabethan England," *History Workshop Journal* 19 (1990): 1–19.

26. William Bradford, *Of Plymouth Plantation* (New York: Random House, 1981), pp. 34–35. For further discussion of this passage in the context of the U.S. Supreme Court decision, see my "Bradford's 'Ancient Members' and 'A Case of Buggery . . . Amongst Them,' " in Andrew Parker, Mary Russo, Doris Sommer, and Patricia Yaeger, eds., *Nationalisms and Sexualities* (New York: Routledge, 1992), pp. 60–76.

27. *The Winthrop Papers,* ed. Steward Mitchell, 5 vols. (Boston: Massachusetts Historical Society, 1929–1947), 2: 205, cited in Michael Warner, "New English Sodom," forthcoming in *American Literature* 64 (1992): 19–47.

28. See Jonathan Katz, *Gay American History,* p. 22, for this passage from Winthrop's *History of New England.*

29. *National Review* 42:13 (July 9, 1990): 16–18.

7.

Multiculturalism and Criticism

JOHN BRENKMAN

1.

Critics, educators, and editorialists have become increasingly embroiled in the debate over multiculturalism. The debate too often misses the essential issues by presuming that multiculturalism is something to be for or against. But whether you look at the United States or Latin America or Africa or most of the countries in Europe and Asia, modern societies *are* multicultural. There are many multiculturalisms. Nigeria, South Africa, India, Brazil, and Yugoslavia do not reduce to a single model. In each case, the peoples who today find their fates linked together within a particular political community have unique histories as well as a specific shared history with each other; they have particular habits and rituals of interaction, and possess evolved, usually conflicting representations of one another—all within a particular set of political institutions and traditions and in the context of particular distributions of power and wealth.

A double task is taking shape for cultural criticism. On the one hand, the multiculturalism of American society has thrown into doubt any appeal to a putatively unified cultural tradition, whether for the purposes of affirmation or critique. A plurality of cultural traditions are active within American society. None of the available constructions of a Western or Anglo-American or American tradition can encompass or sufficiently contextualize the cultural creativity within the United States today. No single stream of tradition furnishes the emergent practices and forms with their shared background. By the same token, then, no individual or social group can legitimately claim to occupy a standpoint from which the whole cultural context can be grasped or, to switch metaphors, to possess as their own the traditions relevant to contemporary cultural production. What then should be the stance and project of a new cultural criticism?

A second task has fallen to those critics committed to, broadly speaking, more egalitarian, libertarian, and pluralistic institutions and practices. For we find ourselves increasingly searching anew the resources of the Western political tradition. There is a need to enrich the idiom of social critique and the vocabulary of democratic commitment. The Marxist tradition has reached an impasse. I do not refer simply to the collapse of communism in Eastern Europe and the Soviet Union. Western Marxism has always distanced itself, even actively disavowed the regimes that used Marxism as a discourse for legitimating power in one-party socialist states. No, the failure of Western Marxism in the revolutions of 1989 and since lay, rather, in the fact that it did not provide—and does not now provide—the social movements in Eastern Europe, the former Soviet Union, or China with the intellectual tools for *their* commitments to more egalitarian, more libertarian, more pluralistic social relations and political institutions. Meanwhile, the forcefulness of Marxist cultural critique in the West has become depleted. The critique of possessive individualism, so consistently the hinge of Marxist interpretations of modern literature and culture (my own included), has not proved capable of generating an alternative conception of individual right and of individual fulfillment. Moreover, the Jacobin and Leninist conception of revolutionary politics has given way to important but still groping experiments with alternative visions of activism and social change.

The two tasks—of taking stock of the multiculturalism of contemporary society and of reviving traditions of radical democracy—are ultimately linked. The multiculturalism of American society is indeed challenging American conceptions of democracy and of the place of diversity in the body politic. As multiculturalism has begun to impinge on education and on contemporary cultural and literary criticism, neoconservative commentators like to blame an imaginary cabal of leftists who have surreptitiously (and unbeknownst to ourselves) taken over academia, hellbent on stirring racial and ethnic animosities. The neoconservatives, ever mindful of tradition and neglectful of history, will not own up to the real reasons multiculturalism has entered the scene so forcefully, namely, because the United States is rife with unsolved social and political problems whose history reaches all the way back to Columbus.

The legacy of conquest, slavery, and racism has yet to become a remote past toward which all Americans might hold a shared perspective. Native American, African American, and Hispanic citizens continue to be denied full participation in the body politic, even as male dominance excluded women from the polity and today threatens their rights anew. Never have our educational institutions made a sustained and concerted effort to ensure that black Americans could retrieve, document, preserve, revive, interpret, and adopt their own history. As new waves of immigrants from Asia, Latin America, and Africa are entering the U.S., legally and illegally, it is crucial to recognize that at many moments in our history, as in the 1920s, citizenship has been impoverished and political participation eroded by racial and ethnic barriers, by the social controls imposed on new immigrants and by the discourses fashioned to justify those barriers and controls. The history of citizenship is also the history of the denial of citizenship.

The multiculturalism controversy includes a dispute over whether this history, part and parcel of American history, should even be taught in the schools. Shall we tell the children about genocide, slavery, racism, xenophobia, imperialism? Neoconservatives don't want the children to know of these evils any more than about the body and sexuality. In the struggle over education the real stakes are the learning processes that will shape citizenship in an increasingly diverse, multi-ethnic, multi-racial society. What is required for young people or immigrants to become not only good citizens, but indeed active citizens? What are the knowledges, the values, the capacities of discussion, organization, deliberation needed for democratic citizenship today? How will we guarantee that all citizens get equal access to the acquiring of these capacities?

Let me spell out my own convictions, since they are the backdrop of the discussion of multiculturalism and democracy that will follow. Citizens can *freely* enter the field of political persuasion and decision only insofar as they draw on the contingent vocabularies of their own identities. Democracy needs participants who are conversant with the images, symbols, stories, and vocabularies that have evolved across the whole of their history. Because of the plurality of such cultural resources and identities in a society like our own, any appeal to the unique validity of a particular cultural tradition is an anti-democratic maneuver.

By the same token, democracy also requires citizens who are fluent enough in *one another's* vocabularies and histories to share the forums of political deliberation and decision on an equal footing. While everyone who enters this agonistic field inevitably deploys their own contingent vocabulary, no one should be able to prevail in political debate and decision without engaging others' contingent vocabularies. What we must learn as critics to understand, and as citizens to practice, and as educators to enable, are these sorts of transfer between the plurality of cultural vocabularies and the necessarily shared discourse of political decision-making. For in a democracy the body politic cannot sustain itself on less variegated traditions than those which nourish the populace it governs.

I am going to develop two lines of argument regarding multiculturalism and democracy, and suggest at the conclusion of each its bearing on cultural and literary criticism. The first line of argument examines the stakes in the neoconservative attack on multiculturalism, and how it threatens important cultural as well as political values. In the second line of argument, I'll discuss how an important tradition of democratic political thought—civic humanism—is transformed when brought into the multicultural context.

2.

It is because neoconservatives fear the broadening of political participation and the deepening of democratic procedures and institutions that they have taken up their attack against multiculturalism.

The destructive direction of neoconservative education reform is clear in twelve years of Reagan-Bush. Their policies have rolled back and threaten to abolish affirmative action in academic admissions and hiring and to increase the spending gap between public and private education, and between urban and suburban schools, with the inevitable result of shoving an ever larger percentage of urban and minority children off the education ladder and depriving immigrant children, especially those who speak Spanish or Chinese, of the skills actually required to integrate into American society. This program of malign neglect uses unequal access to education as a virtual strategy of political disenfranchisement.

The other aim of neoconservatives has been to re-program the intellectual and artistic pursuits of universities, schools, museums, arts councils, and public television. The re-programming has been commanded from the top down through overt and covert government intervention. Yet neoconservatism itself has spawned no new artistic initiatives; it has produced precious little in the way of new interpretive methods in the humanities; and it has scarcely opened any unexplored terrain of scholarly research. Neoconservatism is radically altering our intellectual and artistic institutions by exerting power rather than enhancing knowledge. For more than ten years we have witnessed continual damage visited upon the nation's cultural ecology. William Bennett's tenure at the NEH and the Department of Education was itself a kind of massive oil spill of the mind that has befouled our intellectual shores for years to come.

It is of course Bennett's bully pulpit even more than Allan Bloom's *Closing of the American Mind* that has inspired the rhetoric and intervention of the opponents of multiculturalism like Dinesh D'Souza, Roger Kimball, Donald Kagan, and Joseph Epstein. The debate on multiculturalism in fact represents the belated attempt by the New Right to furnish intellectual justifications for policies and programs that have been mainly driven by a preemptive strike against quite varied intellectual and cultural initiatives. The discourse of anti-multiculturalism represents a serious and worrisome backlash.

It has gotten its polemical bite by taking three phenomena whose import is not in fact at all identical and melding them into a single entity. These phenomena are "political correctness," multiculturalism, and the rejectionist critique of "Western" culture. The neoconservative origins of anti-multiculturalism have not kept it from attracting many liberal intellectuals who in my view will end up seeing their own traditional commitments to equal opportunity, tolerance, and racial integration pulverized in the crucible of neoconservatism. Several contributions to the *New Republic* in 1991, including its special issue on multiculturalism alarmingly entitled "Race on Campus," provide a representative sense of anti-multiculturalism, its characteristic argument and rhetoric and its contradictions. I'll refer in particular to the interventions by Fred Siegel, Edward Rothstein, and Irving Howe, in which liberal discourse slips onto the terrain and into the terms of the neoconservative discourse.

All three of these critics identify multiculturalism with the rejectionist critique of Western culture. All three also tacitly express a yearning for a common culture, an important and frequently progressive aspiration in a society whose divisions and hierarchies have created what Raymond Williams calls the social unevenness of explicit commitment to the notion that this unevenness should be overcome, and that literacy and learning should extend to all segments of society. However, these critics also aspire to have the common culture coincide with the specific cultural experiences they most value and reflectively embrace. It is just that aspiration which contemporary criticism has to give up.

Fred Siegel advances the all-embracing claim that multiculturalism is mired in "political correctness" and totalizing critique. His view of the "number of different radical soils" that have nourished multiculturalism is, though inaccurate, a reliable guide to the current intellectual and political demons of conservative cultural thinking; Foucault and deconstructionism are said to have provided

a new ground for the rejection of Western traditions in toto, and to warrant the search for fundamental philosophical and cultural alternatives, some of which were sought in the cultures that the West has denied or oppressed. And so it was that a vulgarized and oversimplified version of deconstruction joined with black and feminist agendas on campus.

In the same vein, music critic Edward Rothstein starts by attributing to multiculturalism the following reductive view: Western music, like the whole of Western culture, has projected all other cultures as the Other and repudiated them, and that, since music fundamentally "functions as a reinforcement of group identity," democracy dictates that "each culture has an equal right to attention and money for the presentation of its music," while "the tradition of Western music has no essential claim on our attention." Whew, a position well worth rejecting. Fortunately, no one really holds it, as evidenced by Rothstein's failure, duplicated by Howe and typical of the anti-multiculturalists, to identify his antagonists or their writings.

His strawman fluttering in the wind, Rothstein goes on to provide an excellent overview of several recent contributions to ethnomusicology and the study of world music. However, to contrast those musics with Western music he then inverts the parodic portrayal of the multiculturalist view of the Western culture. He asserts that the aesthetic rationality of Western music has given it a unique "will to universality," witnessed by its impact on and absorption of "many folk and religious and courtly . . . traditions":

this impulse to universality helps explain why the West has been so open to the possibilities of other cultures. Though almost all cultures have some interest in the Other, no other culture or tradition, as far as I know, has ever invented something resembling the Western attempt to comprehend the Other through anthropology or ethnomusicology, or has asserted the transcendental perspective through a political vision like Western liberalism or a rational project like Western science.

Valuable work from Edward Said to Mary Louise Pratt and James Clifford having apparently fallen on deaf, if musical, ears, Rothstein's position sets up a false dichotomy. For between the irresponsible (and seldom made) claim that all Western thought is an instrument for the domination of the Other and Rothstein's own uncritical claim that the preoccupation of Western anthropology, music, and politics with the Other has been untouched by the project of Western imperialism there lies a whole complex range of questions, inquiries, and moral-political reflections that have stimulated important work in the humanities since Said's *Orientalism.*

From the standpoint of criticism, Rothstein ends in an untenable dualism. The canon of Western music is to be appreciated and interpreted solely through the categories of its own rationalization of artistic materials and principles, and the resulting understanding is to deem itself, without further scrutiny, participant in a "will to universality." Meanwhile, musics that have emerged from any other society or civilization are to be appreciated and interpreted through the categories of *ethnomusicology,* that is, with an eye to how they are embedded in a wider, though local, network of social practices and communal functions.

This divide, aesthetics on one side and ethnography on the other, is just the split that has been so carefully traversed and rethought in the kind of contemporary cultural theory and criticism that Rothstein, Howe, and Siegel fail to engage. I am thinking, for example, of Pierre Bourdieu and Raymond Williams, whose reflections on the layered yet dynamically interrelated levels of cultural practice in modern societies have not only enriched the study of British and European literature and culture but also demonstrate that every mode of cultural creativity is shaped by its interaction with all of the society's stratifications and differences.

Irving Howe just as dramatically as Rothstein shuts himself off from the task of analyzing these multilayered cultural interactions. Parrying the totalizing critique of the West, he asserts, quite rightly, that

we should want our students to read Shakespeare and Tolstoy, Jane Austen and Kafka, Emily Dickinson and Léopold Senghor, not because they "support" one or another view of social revolution, feminism, and black self-esteem. They don't in many instances; and we don't read them for the sake of enlisting them in a cause of our own. We should want our students to read such writers so that—

and now comes the turn of the *non sequitur,* warding off the possible reflections on colonialism, racism, sexism, and imperialism that this reading list might well invite—

We should want our students to read such writers so that they may learn to enjoy the activity of mind, the pleasure of forms, the beauty of language— in short, the arts in their own right.

I do not believe we should sacrifice the finer-grained connection between artistic forms and social processes. It is essential to reject the notion that the cultivation of understanding and sensitivity to form, thought, and language runs counter to moral-political reflection or the critical interrogation of social structures.

I offer as a kind of credo of the multicultural critic's "job of work" a passage from Adrienne Rich's sequence of poems "North American Time," which comprises a section of her book *Your Native Land, Your Life.* Rich addresses the following poem to herself the writer, but I am taking it in from the standpoint of ourselves as readers and critics:

> Suppose you want to write
> of a woman braiding
> another woman's hair—
> straight down, or with beads and shells
> in three-strand plaits or corn-rows—
> you had better know the thickness
> the length——the pattern
> why she decides to braid her hair
> how it is done to her

what country it happens in
what else happens in that country

You have to know these things

Reading pulls us toward moments where structures and institutions are shown as they take hold within human experience as everyday habits, practices, rituals. Literature gives us glimpses of the element in which social relationships are conducted, with or against the grain. Perhaps the two women are secretly lovers, and the one does the other's hair so that some token of their hidden desire can display itself in the world. Perhaps the pattern of the braid and the beads and shells are meant to defy the gaze of a community or its expectations or its values. Perhaps the corn-rows are for a woman who is white and wealthy and is having her hair done in a black woman's beauty parlor. Perhaps a mother is winding her reluctant, growing daughter's hair into pigtails in an anxious defense against time, or from a fear of sexuality, or in alarmed awareness of her daughter's vulnerability. Suppose you want to write criticism—to read any one of these gestures as you might encounter them in a poem or novel is to become entangled in social and political realities, not as duty or homage to an ideology but as a response to words, situated, used, needed words.

Multiculturalism is radically altering the situation, use, and need of words. Many fear cacophony. Transformations of the language unsettle. People tend to peg their very sense of social solidarity on a commonality of language. The charging of words with new connotations is probably not disturbing in itself, but what is disturbing is the cause of those new connotations, namely, that the language is being deployed in new contexts and is relaying new interactions and new social relationships. Such social and cultural transformations are at work in literature, not apart from it. Criticism will hardly "save literature" by retreating from the resulting tasks of social analysis and political reflection.

3.

A democracy in the contemporary world cannot create a monocultural citizenry. And yet a multicultural citizenry cannot generate a polity solely on the basis of its differences. There are inescapable tensions in the relationship between multiculturalism and democracy. What resources does the Western political tradition offer to make those tensions productive rather than destructive?

Several European theorists (Claude Lefort, Chantal Mouffe, François Furet) and English-language theorists like Carole Pateman, Michael Walzer, and Charles Taylor have revisited civic republicanism as an alternative to the more prevalent strand of modern democratic theory, liberalism. Civic republicanism or civic humanism, the "Machiavellian moment" in J.G.A. Pocock's phrase, furnishes a rich picture of the self-governing community. Unlike liberalism, it does not conceptualize an intrinsic connection between democracy and capitalism. It offers a positive rather than negative definition of freedom, and it construes citizenship as a many-sided activity based on active political participation in contrast to, for example, Locke's liberal stress on freedom for private pursuits. Republicanism normatively projects citizens who are equals in ruling and being ruled. Moreover, the republican ideal of citizenship does not posit an intrinsic antagonism between individuals' self-assertion or pursuit of their own interests and their commitment to the common good; personal fulfillment is interwoven with civic commitment.

The tradition's essential tenet has been formulated by Pocock in the following terms:

Civic humanism denotes a style of thought . . . in which it is contended that the development of the individual toward self-fulfillment is possible only when the individual acts as a citizen, that is as a conscious and autonomous participant in an autonomous decision-taking community, a polis or republic.

For all the promise of its vision of civic participation as an alternative to liberalism's privatism and for all its resonance throughout American history, civic humanism also always assumed the homogeneity of those who enjoyed citizenship. As Michael Warner has shown, for example, the republican representation of citizenship in revolutionary America tacitly depended upon the exclusion of women, African slaves, and Native Americans from the forms of literacy that were the emblem and the means of the patriots' equality. To evoke the republican tradition in the context of multicultural societies quickly exposes those elements of civic humanism that run directly counter to diversity and plurality.

This predicament should be a reminder that the development of modern society is as much a challenge to Western political traditions as a continuation of them. As Claude Lefort and François Furet have argued, the French Revolution introduced into modern political culture the explosive possibility for *all* members of society to lay claim to citizenship. If the republican tradition is to be a resource of democracy in a multicultural society, its conception of citizenship will have to be rethought. Many are the themes for such a rethinking—the role of *property;* the sources of civic *virtue;* the model of *historical process*—but I will here focus only on the theme of property in order to suggest the kinds of transformation required in critically redeeming civic humanism as a political vocabulary.

Classical civic humanism tied citizenship to property. The citizen was always envisioned as a property-owner. Modern democracy has not of course continued to impose such a limit on political participation. The illegitimacy of the property requirement has been recognized, slowly, through the extension of suffrage to workers, women, and finally blacks. The tradition's ideal of citizens as equals in ruling and being ruled rested on the implicit sense they were already on a par with one another within the larger fabric of social relations. Classical civic humanism always defined citizenship with reference to just one form of ownership and thus to just one social role: the master of the household in ancient Athens; the Medieval freeholder-warrior; the American farmer-patriot.

The assumption of structurally stable social spaces is altogether incompatible with modern democracy. The effects of universal suffrage do not simply enlarge the polis. Carole Pateman has shown that women's suffrage, for example, had effects far beyond the extension of basic citizenship rights to women; the participation of women in politics has disturbed and altered the structured separation of public and private spheres, a separation that has been a linchpin of various social and political institutions. As new arenas of political participation are opened, and as new citizens participate, social changes occur following a dynamic quite alien to the self-mirroring equality of premodern citizenship.

More generally, as Ernesto Laclau and Chantal Mouffe have argued, individuals carry out a complex of social roles. They participate in many types of social relations and have identities shaped, and reshaped, by varied activities and associations. The position from which citizens become actively engaged in political deliberation and decision is neither permanent nor predictable. Modern citizenship does not rest upon just one role or identity; it gets articulated, rather, via several, mutable paths of social relationships and identity. When neoconservatives or liberals today evoke the supposed homogeneity required for democratic citizenship, they are not only swimming against the stream of our own society's history, they are constrained increasingly to define that homogeneity as mere ideological conformity rather than as active consent. In response we must define and defend the equality, not the homogeneity, of citizens in the context of multiculturalism.

An unexpected resource lies within another fold in the meaning of property in civic humanism. There is an important value embedded in the tie between citizenship and property, a value that will have to be reinterpreted not merely recovered. Property anchored citizenship in republican ideology, especially with reference to the Medieval freeholder-warrior and the American farmer-patriot, because it gave individuals the social basis of their *independence*. A source of the virtue that enabled the citizen's commitment to the common good was the independence he had achieved through his livelihood. The "Gothic" freeholder was outside the web of dependence between vassals and lords and that between the lords and the crown. Similarly, patriotic farmers became American archetypes for individuals ready for self-government among equals.

Leaving aside how compromised these ideals or archetypes were in their actual societies, virtue and equality cannot begin or end with property in the modern polity. Indeed, the social bases of American citizens are diverse, and their relations of dependence are multiple. How then is the value of independence to be retrieved against the grain of the republican tradition? It requires a different foundation and different guarantees. Rethought from a modern perspective, the civic humanist tradition reminds us that individuals are not free to act as citizens unless their own most basic security and welfare are not at risk. Poverty debilitates citizenship, just as assuredly as property once secured it. Moreover, independence requires that individuals' free exercise of their powers of political participation be protected against those upon whom they are socially dependent: tenants vis-à-vis landlords, employees vis-à-vis employers, welfare clients vis-à-vis government agencies or social authorities, frequently women vis-à-vis men.

To revive civic humanism in the context of political modernity is, therefore, to transform it. Republican ideals have to be loosed from their proprietary forms to be salvaged at all. The body politic has to be reimagined as an arena in which political participation stimulates social change rather than confirming existing relations and institutions. Citizenship has to embrace equality without demanding homogeneity, in keeping with the diversity of social roles characteristic of modern societies. And the value of independence has to be transformed into a mesh of legal and moral protections to guarantee active political participation.

The building-blocks or enabling conditions of citizenship are not the same in 1992 as they were in 1776, or at least the means of acquiring and preserving them have altered radically. Full citizenship requires voting rights and constitutional protections, of course; it also requires education in the skills of active political participation. Those are requirements for the individual looked at separately and therefore somewhat abstractly. For the conflicts over citizenship that have been important historically and are alive yet today involve the enabling conditions by which social groups acquire citizenship. The relevant building-blocks themselves have to be secured politically. They become objects of struggle, in contrast to the classical tradition's image of the republic achieving its final, perfected form in the moment of its founding. From the standpoint of the social group, citizenship requires adequate political representation; jobs and access to the full range of the society's economic activities; and the material and institutional means needed to participate in the forming of public opinion. The neoconservative and neoliberal mania for insisting that all questions regarding citizenship merely concern individuals as individuals, not as members of social groups, is a bid to forestall struggles over these *social* requirements of citizenship.

Is participation in the polity mediated through membership in a group or anchored in the individual's rights and social contract? Versions of this question underlie virtually every discussion of multiculturalism in the American context. As Peter H. Schuck and Rogers M. Smith have shown, American legal thinking and policy regarding immigrants and racial minorities have unfolded in the tension between ascriptive and consensual conceptions of citizenship, that is, between birthright and contract.

In *Beyond Ethnicity,* Werner Sollors richly details the polarity of descent and consent in American discourse on identity, ethnicity, nation, citizenship. *Consent* stresses how one's identity is self-made and one's social and political participation contractual, while *descent* according to Sollors values ancestral identifications and hereditary ties. These contrary "definitions of American identity" are, he argues, "the central drama in American culture. Consent and descent are terms which allow me to approach and question the whole maze of American ethnicity and culture." I do not think this claim really accords with the dense patterns of themes, symbols, and narratives that Sollors so compellingly teases out and then arrays along the axis of consent and descent.

Whereas Sollors takes this web of consent and descent as the meaning of the American discourse on ethnicity, I take it to be something like the language or the constraining grammar in which the American discourse on ethnicity gets articulated. The actual meaning of those articulations cannot be determined with reference to the semantic grid of descent and consent itself. Because Sollors does not examine what the actual conditions of a group's citizenship are when it takes up the discourse on identity, because he does not look to the pattern by which its members' citizenship was denied or curtailed, he creates the false impression that every group in American history has confronted the dialectic of ethnicity and citizenship in a comparable way.

Consider, though, that blacks were historically not merely excluded from the American polity; they were inscribed within it as *non-participants*. The forms of that negating inscription have varied through a complex history of legal and political designations. These set the conditions of the African American discourse on identity and citizenship, and the meaning of that discourse would in turn have to be interpreted in light of those conditions and of the strategies embodied in its response to them. Slavery, Dred Scott, the Fugitive Slave law, Jim Crow, and so on, down to the current disenfranchisement through poverty and unequal access, give African Americans a specific history in the polity. How that history affects African American forms of solidarity or identity or political participation has to be analyzed with reference to these specific distortions of the American polity, not just the grid of descent and consent.

Lacking this perspective, the interpretations of descent and consent risk becoming tautological. The orientation to politically charged group identity is viewed invariably as a product of the narratives of descent. But this is misleading on two counts. It misses the ways in which group identity responds to the institutional and discursive organization of "consent," that is, the prevailing consensus governing the body politic. Second, Sollors's consistent association of ethnic or racial identity with "descent" stems in part from the tendentious definition he gives descent in the first place. He categorizes inheritance, heritage, legacy in the cultural sense with heredity in the biological sense. Descent always has an aura of regression, irrationality, or fictionality about it in Sollors's interpretations because every narrative of heritage, every symbol of solidarity, every theme of historical belonging looks like a variant of biology and heredity.

Surely, as Sollors argues, heritages and collective histories are *constructions,* but not in a manner that is intrinsically different from the way other aspects of social relationships are discursively or symbolically constructed—including consent. The mythic moment in our understanding of consent is that only the individual, as individual, gives consent to the polis and receives its consent in turn. Individuals in fact participate in the polis as culturally and socially shaped agents, just as they are barred from the polis on the basis of their group belonging. Likewise, as I have argued with reference to civic humanism, the modern polity is a dynamic space in which citizenship is always being contested rather than the fixed space of the premodern ideal of a republic. "Consent," too, is contested, which means that neither the polis nor the individual is so purely autonomous as social contract theory tends to suppose.

I want to close by again stressing how the modernity and the multiculturalism of our own polity affect the stance and project of literary and cultural criticism. Earlier I argued that literary forms arise in interaction with the socially stratified and culturally differentiated practices of the society as a whole. Indeed, aspects of multiculturalism suggest that it is in the "intercultural" spaces that the "culture" is actually created. By the same token, the discussion of consent and descent is a reminder that a people's history and the evolution of its expressive forms are neither mere heredity nor arbitrary construction. Literary forms, like all cultural practices, are embedded or situated in collective histories.

How, though, should criticism square the recognition that texts (and readers) are socially situated with the need to create new spaces of a shared culture and polity?

One direction critics have taken to solve this question has been the idea of "positionality" on a grid of "gender, race, and class." Beyond its un-

deniable value as an indicator of the sorts of social relations that shape
cultural production and reception, the idea of positionality often aspires to
a more comprehensive theoretical role. It takes on the task of synthesizing
the double perspective of shared standpoint and cultural plurality. The
reference to a shared, or potentially shared, standpoint lies in the tacit
appeal to an ultimate overcoming of hierarchies of gender, race and class.
Meanwhile, the situatedness of reader or text is defined by its "position"
within the gender-race-class grid.

Its heuristic value notwithstanding, the gender-race-class grid has several
flaws as a "theory." First, it appeals to what Walzer calls "simple equality."
It postulates an end to gender, race, and class inequalities without acknowledging that equality does not have a universal or unequivocal meaning
when it comes to determining what a just distribution of different social
goods actually is. The meanings of equality cannot be settled by theory in
the first place, but only through processes of political conflict, deliberation,
and decision.

A second flaw lies in the tendency to assume that the gridded "position"
of a reader or text determines outlook, meaning, or identity. The identification of one's social location solely in these terms leads to what Nancy
K. Miller has called "as a" criticism. A critic might, for example, position
himself "*as a* white heterosexual middle-class male. . . ." It seems to me
that if you feel compelled to speak *as* a "white heterosexual middle-class
male . . .," you would do better just to keep your mouth shut. Nor can
the social constraints that limit or warp one's knowledge and values be
magically overturned simply by pinpointing one's own, or another's, supposed "position" in a social structure.

"Positionality" is perhaps the wrong abstraction for determining the
socially and politically relevant aspects of identity-formation. It misses the
crucial difficult and productive tension within every position, namely, that
we are always at one and the same time a member of——(or participant
in——) *and* a citizen. Moreover, gender-race-class positionality too easily
misses the conflicts that arise *within* every identifiable social group and
manifest themselves in *its* political-cultural debates over its identity, its
guiding values, its strategies of struggle, its visions of the community's
most desired and its most feared destiny. Stepping into the fray is what
criticism is all about.

WORKS CITED

Arendt, Hannah. *The Human Condition.* Chicago: University of Chicago Press, 1958.
Bloom, Allan. *The Closing of the American Mind.* New York: Simon and Schuster, 1987.
Bourdieu, Pierre. *Distinction: A Social Critique of the Judgement of Taste.* Trans. Richard Nice.
    Cambridge, Mass.: Harvard University Press, 1984.

Clifford, James and George E. Marcus, eds. *Writing Culture: The Poetics and Politics of Ethnography*. Berkeley and Los Angeles: University of California Press, 1986.

Furet, François. *Interpreting the French Revolution*. Trans. Elborg Forster. Cambridge: Cambridge University Press, 1981.

Howe, Irving. "The Value of the Canon." *New Republic* (February 18, 1991), pp. 40–47.

Hutchinson, E.P. *Legislative History of American Immigration Policy, 1798–1965*. Philadelphia: University of Pennsylvania Press, 1981.

Laclau, Ernesto and Chantal Mouffe. *Hegemony and Socialist Strategy: Towards a Radical Democratic Politics*. Trans. Winston Moore and Paul Cammack. London: Verso, 1985.

Lefort, Claude. *The Political Forms of Modern Society: Bureaucracy, Democracy, Totalitarianism*. Ed. John B. Thompson. Cambridge, Mass.: MIT Press, 1986.

Michaels, Walter Benn. "The Souls of White Folk." *Literature and the Body: Essays on Populations and Persons*. Selected Essays of the English Institute, 1986. Ed. Elaine Scarry. Baltimore: The Johns Hopkins University Press, 1988. 185–209.

————."The Vanishing American." *American Literary History*. 2:2 (Summer 1990): 220–241.

Miller, Nancy K. *Getting Personal: Feminist Occasions and Other Autobiographical Acts*. New York: Routledge, 1991.

Mouffe, Chantal. "Radical Democracy: Modern or Postmodern." *Universal Abandon? The Politics of Postmodernism*. Ed. Andrew Ross. Minneapolis: University of Minnesota Press, 1988.

Pateman, Carole. *The Sexual Contract*. Stanford: Stanford University Press, 1988.

————.*The Disorder of Women: Democracy, Feminism and Political Theory*. Stanford: Stanford University Press, 1989.

Pocock, J.G.A. *The Machiavellian Moment: Florentine Political Thought and the Atlantic Republican Tradition*. Princeton: Princeton University Press, 1975.

————.*Virtue, Commerce, and History*. Cambridge: Cambridge University Press, 1985.

————.*Politics, Language and Time: Essays on Political Thought and History*. Chicago: University of Chicago Press, 1989 [1971].

Rich, Adrienne. *Your Native Land, Your Life*. New York: Norton, 1986.

Rothstein, Edward. "Roll Over Beethoven." *New Republic*. February 4, 1991. 29–34.

Said, Edward. *Orientalism*. New York: Pantheon, 1978.

Schuck, Peter H. and Rogers M. Smith. *Citizenship without Consent: Illegal Aliens in the American Polity*. New Haven: Yale University Press, 1985.

Shapiro, Ian. *Political Criticism*. Berkeley and Los Angeles: University of California Press, 1990.

Siegel, Fred. "The Cult of Multiculturalism." *New Republic*. February 18, 1991. 34–40.

Sollors, Werner. *Beyond Ethnicity: Consent and Descent in American Culture*. New York: Oxford University Press, 1986.

Taylor, Charles. *Philosophy and the Human Sciences: Philosophical Papers, 2*. Cambridge: Cambridge University Press, 1985.

————."Invoking Civil Society." Working Papers. Chicago: Center for Psychosocial Studies, 1990.

Walzer, Michael. *Spheres of Justice: A Defense of Pluralism and Equality*. New York: Basic Books, 1983.

Warner, Michael. *The Letters of the Republic: Publication and the Public Sphere in Eighteenth-Century America*. Cambridge, Mass.: Harvard University Press, 1990.

8.

The Unbearable Ugliness of Volvos

STANLEY FISH

On a day in the mid-seventies—it may have varied in different parts of the country and at different universities—American academics stopped buying ugly Volkswagens and started buying ugly Volvos, with a few nonconformists opting for ugly Saabs. Now on the surface there would seem to be an obvious explanation for this shift in preference: on the one hand, graduate student stipends gave way to the more generous salaries of assistant and associate professorships; on the other, growing families required more than a rudimentary backseat. But the question remains, why Volvos; why not Oldsmobiles, or Chryslers, or Mercury station wagons? The answer I think is that Volvos provided a solution to a new dilemma facing many academics—how to enjoy the benefits of increasing affluence while at the same time maintaining the proper attitude of disdain toward the goods affluence brings. In the context of this dilemma, the ugliness of the Volvo becomes its most attractive feature for it allows those who own one to plead innocent of the charge of really wanting it. There must be another reason for the purchase, in this case a reason provided conveniently by the manufacturer in an advertising strategy that emphasizes safety. We don't buy these big expensive luxurious cars because we want to be comfortable or (God forbid) ostentatious; we buy them because we want to be safe. (I can only guess how many academics are now gobbling up overpriced Michelin tires reassured by a recent advertising campaign that they are purchasing family security rather than performance or glamor.) The ugliness of the automobile makes the cashing in of its negative value a straightforward and *immediate* transaction. Were the car not ugly, a Volvo owner might be in danger of hearing someone say, "My, what a stunning Volvo," to which he or she would have to respond, "Well, perhaps, but I really bought it because it is safe." But no Volvo owner will ever face the challenge of an unwanted compliment, and therefore the disclaimer of non-utilitarian motives need not even be made. Of course this entire economy is now threatened by the revelation that tests demonstrating Volvo's superior safety were faked; but since they are mostly academics, Volvo owners will no doubt be resourceful in the search for rationalizations and will probably take comfort from *Consumer Reports* or some other publication that breathes the proper anti-commercial virtue.

Now it might be said that the relationship between academics and their Volvos is not exactly central to the life of the academy; but in fact it seems to me emblematic of a basic academic practice, the practice of translating into the language of higher motives desires and satisfactions one is unable or unwilling to acknowledge. If I can put the matter in the form of a rule or rule of thumb: whenever you either want something or get something, manage it in such a way as to deny or disguise its material pleasures. Nor is this a rule simply of *personal* behavior; it can generate the behavior of the entire profession. Consider, for example, the very material pleasures of the lecture and conference circuit, something that was not in place when I was a graduate student in the late fifties and early sixties. The flourishing of the circuit has brought with it new sources of extra income, increased opportunities for domestic and foreign travel, easy access to national and international centers of research, an ever-growing list of stages on which to showcase one's talents, and geometric increase in the availability of the commodities for which academics yearn, attention, applause, fame, and ultimately, adulation of a kind usually reserved for the icons of popular culture. In the face of such a cornucopia of benefits the academic world is in danger of at once providing and experiencing unadulterated gratification, but (never fear) the danger is warded off by a set of practices that exacts a payment, usually in advance, for every potential pleasure. Nine times out of ten when you arrive in a strange city there will be no one to meet you despite elaborate and repeated promises, or, if you are met, you will be taken to a hotel only to find that the reservations were never made and every room is taken, or if the reservations have been made and there is a room, the hotel is in the course of being rebuilt (this seems to be a requirement for hotels at the MLA convention) and there is no possibility at all of either sleep or study. And if these difficulties are somehow overcome or avoided, and you actually get to the campus at the appointed time, more or less prepared, the room you are supposed to speak in will be locked and no one will know who has the key; and if the room isn't locked, it will be occupied by a scheduled class; or if it is unoccupied, it will either be impossibly small or embarrassingly large; or if by some accident it is the right size, it will be the only room in the university, if not the entire state, that is un-air-conditioned. You will then be introduced by someone who takes pride in either forgetting or mispronouncing your name, who associates you with work you haven't done in ten years, who attributes to you opinions the reverse of those you actually hold, and who believes that it is only by a perverse turn of fate that he or she is not being introduced by *you*. The audience you then address will be a fraction of what it might have been had the lecture or panel been properly advertised; there will be insufficient time for questions and discussion; and when it is all over, and you have endured a dinner only slightly less adversarial than your Ph.D. orals, you are then left alone, at 7:45 p.m., to pass the long night in a town that offers you only a passing parade of unfamiliar faces.

Transposed to another institutional key, the same scenario plays itself out in the context of the job market. Here the visit is to a potential employer, but it often seems that you are interviewing for a place in a penal colony. Again, the arrangements are systematically botched; planes not met, reservations mixed up; rather than being introduced by someone who barely knows your name, you are interrogated by deans who mistake you for the candidate from neurosurgery; your schedule is a brutal one in the course of which you meet potential future colleagues who warn you away from their territory even as they try to enlist you in wars now going into their twentieth year; you have coffee with students who inform you that you were the department's fourth choice; later you will have an intimate dinner with department members whose inability to talk to you is exceeded only by their inability to talk to each other. At your presentation or, rather, audition, you will be asked many questions, but the content of all of them will be the same: what makes you think that you're good enough to join us in the first place? Finally you leave town without ever having had a chance to find out very much about the things that would really be of concern to anyone contemplating relocating from one place to another; and in general it seems that no one thought to ask the most obvious question: if I were coming to see whether I wished to exchange my present situation for a new one, what would I want to know and how would I want to be treated?

The result is perfectly in line with the general rule I announced earlier: the pleasure and satisfaction of landing a new and better job is blunted and even overwhelmed by the programmatic unpleasantness of the process. Nor is this an accident that could be avoided if a few obvious truths about social and human obligations were pointed out to the responsible parties; for the inattentiveness, like the ugliness of Volvos, is *purposeful* and is valued both by those who perform it and those who receive it; for were the process to be efficient and sensitive both to the personal feelings of the participants and to the realities of the marketplace, it would be too much like the world of business, and the investment in being distinguishable from business is so great that academics will pay any price to protect it.

In the collective eye of the academy, sloppiness, discourtesy, indifference, and inefficiency are *virtues,* signs of an admirable disdain for the mere surfaces of things, a disdain that is itself a sign of a dedication to higher, if invisible, values. Once one understands this an otherwise puzzling feature of academic life makes perfect sense. I am referring to the remarkably uniform incompetence of academic administrators. It is tempting to say, as many have, that academics get the administrators they deserve, but it would be more accurate to say that academics get the administrators they *want.* What they want is administrators who are either so weak that they provide no protection against the pressures exerted by higher-level administrators or so tyrannical that there is no protection against the pressures *they* exert. In either case, by getting the administrators they want, academics get what they *really* want—they get to be downtrodden; and by getting to be downtrodden, academics get what they really *really* want—they get to complain. If one listens to academics, one might make the mistake of thinking they would like their complaints to be remedied; but in fact the complaints of academics are their treasures, and were you to remove them, you would find either that they had been instantly replenished or that you were now their object. The reason that academics want and need their complaints is that it is important to them to feel oppressed, for in the psychic economy of the academy, oppression is the sign of virtue. The more victimized you are, the more subject to various forms of humiliation, the more you can tell yourself that you are in the proper relation to the corrupted judgment of merely worldly eyes. Were you to be rewarded in accordance with what you took to be your true worth, that worth would immediately be suspect. The sense of superiority so characteristic of the academic mentality requires for its maintenance continued evidence of the world's disdain, evidence that takes the form of poor working conditions, the elimination of so-called privileges like offices and telephones, increases in course loads, decreases in salary, and public ridicule. As each of these misfortunes is visited upon the academic, he or she acquires a greater measure of that pained sensitivity that makes so many academic faces indistinguishable from the faces of medieval martyrs.

Now if martyrdom and self-denial, even self-hatred, are the true treasures of the academic life, it follows that the generous academic will be eager to share those treasures with others. That is the purpose of tenure decisions and other rites of academic passage. Here the skill is once again to manage the bestowing of rewards in such a way as to render them bitter to the taste. The strategies include delay, ritual humiliations, unannounced shifts in standards, procedures that are either frustratingly secret or painfully public. The meetings themselves are an exercise in virtuoso captiousness where the art is to find the formulation that will best express the proper combination of regretful compassion and condemnation: "a great teacher, an excellent colleague, but . . . ." "The work is good and there is an impressive amount of it, but. . . ." "We have no better undergraduate teacher, but. . . ." And if there seems to be nothing to fault, there is always the invocation of the standard that no one, least of all the invoker, could meet: "Is she taking the field in an entirely new direction?" And if the answer should be "yes," it is no trick at all to turn it into a negative. "Is her work so ahead of the field that no one will be inclined to follow her?"

You get the idea; you've been getting and giving it all your life, when you've been blocked from teaching a course for so long that when you are finally assigned it, you are no longer interested in the material, when you've waited for years for an office you're given three months before the building is torn down, when you've been an associate professor for so long that promotion can only be experienced as an insult. Whatever else they are, academics are resourceful and when they set their minds to it, there are no limits to the varieties of pain they can inflict on one another.

Originally I had intended to write this paper differently, not as an unfolding argument, but as a simple enumeration of the aphorisms I have been fashioning since I entered the profession in 1962. Here is a sample:

—*In the academy, the lower the act, the higher the principle invoked to justify it.* This aphorism underlies the analyses I offered earlier; it speaks to the academic inability to acknowledge desire unless it is packaged as altruism. It also speaks to the bizarre but strangely logical outcome of this transformative practice: pettiness, which might be held in check were it acknowledged for what it is, instead becomes raised to a principle, and is renamed eccentricity or even individualism so that it can then be defended in the name of academic freedom. In this way acts of incredible cruelty can be licensed and even admired. The sequence leads us to another aphorism:

—*academics like to keep their eyes on the far horizon with the result that everything and everyone in the near horizon gets sacrificed.* The curious thing is that academics like to sacrifice themselves; that is,

—*academics like to feel morally culpable especially in relation to those who would give anything to be in their place;* and also

—*academics like to feel morally superior, which they manage by feeling morally culpable.* (Together these aphorisms illuminate a curious history in which already enfranchised academics, largely male, gazed with envy and strangely mediated desire at the disenfranchised, first at Jews, then at women, then at blacks, and then at Native Americans, and now at gays and Arabs.)

Let me emphasize again that these aphorisms describe a two-way commerce, victim and victimizer, trashers and trashees, each not only needing, but desiring the other. The essence of it all is contained in the very first aphorism I ever formulated, in 1964 as I watched my colleagues at Berkeley turn from abasing themselves before deans and boards of trustees to abasing themselves before students. Here is the aphorism:—*Academics like to eat shit and in a pinch, they don't care whose shit they eat.* Of course had I known enough at the time, I could have saved myself the trouble and simply quoted from Freud's essays on masochism. For the masochist, Freud explains, "it is the suffering itself that matters; whether the sentence is cast by a loved one or by an indifferent person is of no importance; it may even be caused by impersonal forces or circumstances, but the true masochist always holds out his cheek whenever he sees a chance of receiving a blow" ("The Economic Problem in Masochism," in *General Psychological Theory,* p. 196). (A friend suggested to me that a better title for this essay might be "An Academic Is Being Beaten.")

In the past year many blows have been struck and many cheeks have been proffered. The always-dormant strain of anti-intellectualism in American life has been reawakened by a virulent union of disgruntled neoconservatives and ignorant journalists. In nearly every newspaper and magazine in the country, teachers of literature have been credited with the destruction of Western Civilization and with other nameless crimes. Academic-bashing has become the national spectator sport, and, predictably, some academics are among the best players. They may soon be outdistanced, however, by a growing chorus of politicians led by George Bush who have realized anew what Ronald Reagan found in the 1966 California gubernatorial election, that academics present an irresistible target, not simply because they are highly visible but because, by and large, they will not fight back. The election year of 1992 promises to provide a perfect match of an attacking army and a target population that finds its pleasure in punishment. Before it is all over both sides may be moved to echo Wordsworth: "bliss was it in those times to be alive."

Of course, I may be wrong; it may not go that way. Indeed everything that I have said may be wrong or worse, which is why, despite the fifty-year tradition of the English Institute, I would prefer not to entertain questions at the conclusion of this paper. Instead, and in accordance with the spirit of academic practice, I will cheerfully plead guilty to all charges in advance. I acknowledge that the statements I have made are too sweeping and admit of innumerable exceptions; that some Volvos are beautiful; that no one here now owns or has ever owned a Volvo; that the life you experience in your various departments is characterized by generosity; and that your relationship to the rewards and privileges of the profession is straightforward and healthy. I further acknowledge that I am necessarily (and multiply) implicated in the critique I have presented, that I have been a member of the academy for thirty years in which I have been an eager participant in its economy, often providing, as I have here, the desired beating for those who have assembled to receive it, that every sin of which I have accused others is *writ large* in my own performance. And finally I acknowledge that there is no justification whatsoever for that performance, that it is irresponsible, self-indulgent, self-aggrandizing, and entirely without redeeming social or intellectual value. It is just something I have always wanted to do.

9.

Preaching to the Converted

GERALD GRAFF

At the first meeting of the English Institute in 1939, an observer noted that there seemed "to have developed a loss of confidence in old tasks and old ways of performing them . . . ."[1] I suspect that by comparison with our state of upheaval a half century later, what seemed like a loss of confidence in 1939 would seem like rock-like self-assurance today. Even so, I think a foreshadowing of our current agitations can be detected in the less noisy climate of half a century ago. 1939 was, after all, a critical historical moment, with the end of a depression and the start of a world war. It was a moment when the American university, caught up in the democratizing effects of these events, was entering the great transition into a mass educational institution that would culminate in the postwar multiversity. In such a climate, it was easy to lose confidence in a humanities research industry whose interests were already suspected of being too minutely specialized and esoteric to justify itself educationally and socially.

The postwar leap in enrollment, which would eventually bring over half the eligible American population into American colleges, raised questions about the public value of academic knowledge-production that put academic humanists especially on the defensive. Exactly why humanists should want or need to do specialized research had seemed mysterious from the beginnings of the research university in the 1880s, not just to people outside the academy but to the humanists' colleagues in the sciences. Humanities research had seemed to do no great harm, however, as long as the average university enrolled fewer than five thousand students and most English departments consisted of two or three professors and a handful of graduate students. But as the size and cost of the academic operation increased, the stakes were raised in the commerce between the academy and the larger culture, and the costs of academic malpractice were magnified. The postwar expansion of the academy intensified the pressures on the humanities research enterprise, which was increasingly expected to justify itself in terms that the general public could appreciate and was less likely to be excused when it could not.

We need to keep this historical background in mind when we consider the recent wave of attacks on the academic humanities for their new habit of asking unpleasant political questions about supposedly apolitical subjects like literature, criticism, and composition. Today's attack on tenured and untenured radicals would not be so powerful if it did not tap into a much older set of suspicions that took root long before any feminist or poststructuralist critics were dreamed of. The attacks on the current state of the academic humanities are powerful because they build on uncertainties that have existed since the advent of the modern research university, uncertainties about what it is that academic humanists do when they are not correcting students' grammar and spelling and why it should be supported by taxpayers, donors, and tuition-paying students.

This is not to minimize the remarkable difference in tone between the satiric news items on academic literature conventions that had been published for decades and the recent ones attacking "political correctness." Whereas these articles still exploit the comedy of pedantic or opaque paper titles, they no longer project the old reassuring image of professors as lovable fuddy-duddies comically unable to extricate themselves from their footnotes and subordinate clauses. On top of our time-honored reputation for being incomprehensible we have acquired a new reputation for being politically obnoxious—some even claim we have managed the difficult feat of being both at once.

The philistine anti-intellectualism to which the recent attacks appeal is disturbing enough, and I do not intend to say anything to appease it. One does not need to give aid and comfort to philistinism, however, to point out that the humanities have often made themselves easy targets for such attacks by adopting an attitude of lofty indifference to their public image. Academic humanists have always been slow to recognize the widespread public uncertainties about what it is they do, what their research is all about, and why it should be supported by institutions devoted to educating undergraduates. Or, if they have recognized these uncertainties, they have preferred on the whole to treat them as inevitable rather than to make much effort to clear them up.

To be sure, humanists can point out, often rightly enough, that it is in the nature of their research that it will not necessarily have direct application to undergraduate teaching, that much of most important research could not be done at all if it had to translate its terms at all times into sound bites accessible to a wide public. Unfortunately, such justifications often serve to excuse complacency about the research enterprise, just as objections to sound-bite communication excuse the failure to express ideas clearly. It seems reasonable to demand that if academic scholarship hopes for strong public support, it be able to justify itself in educational terms and make its rationale accessible to the public at the level of competent journalism. Yet many humanists still react with querulous resistance to such a demand, as if our public and even our students had no business prying into our professional affairs. This indifference to public accountability does not become any more attractive when it comes from academic progressives instead of traditionalists.

It seems the academic humanities have yet to come to terms with the fact that once the university became a mass institution, it perforce became an agent of cultural popularization. Even those academics who study and promote popular culture still often think of the popularization of their own analyses as inherently vulgar. No academic is comfortable at being called a "popularizer," and few would readily accept the suggestion that a humanities department is in an important sense as much a form of "popular culture" as are television stations and newspapers. Yet the academy is in a certain sense a branch of show business, a "society of spectacle," as Geoffrey Hartman put it in his talk yesterday. After all, what else is an institution that proffers its ideas and interpretations to a nationwide constituency of millions if it is not a form of popular culture? If we are *not* would-be popularizers of the texts and ideas we talk about, what then is our relation to those masses of undergraduates who turn up in our courses? The reluctance to acknowledge that what we do has a show business dimension only makes it more likely that we will be *bad* show business. Not that acknowledging that you are a branch of show business necessarily makes you any better at it, but it does seem a step in the direction of taking some responsibility for how you represent yourself publicly.

There are some signs that the present culture war is shaking us out of this complacency and forcing humanists to recognize that we too are part of the culture industry and are in a critical struggle for our voice in it. If this is the result of the hostilities, we may be able to look back at some point on even the most ill-informed and malicious attacks on the academy and say, "Thanks, we needed that." Whatever else one may say about these recent attacks, their success with the media and the public has exposed something that we cannot afford to ignore, namely, how poorly we academic humanists have carried out our role as agents of cultural popularization.

In a powerful response to the critics of "political correctness" in the *Village Voice,* Michael Bérubé observes that "public discussion of American academia is now conducted by the most callow and opportunistic elements of the Right." He notes that "recent literary theory is so rarely accorded the privilege of representing itself in non-academic forums that journalists, disgruntled professors, embittered ex-graduate students and their families and friends now feel entitled to say anything at all about the academy without fear of contradiction by general readers. The field is wide open and there's no penalty for charlatanism (quite the contrary), since few general readers are informed enough to spot even the grossest forms of misrepresentation and fraud.''[2] I agree wholly with Bérubé, but I think it needs to be added that we academic humanists bear a good deal of responsibility for the situation he describes. Having disdained popular self-representation, we have predictably been inept in representing ourselves in the public sphere and thus made ourselves easy prey for those who would ignorantly or maliciously misrepresent us. Having treated mere image-making as beneath our dignity, we have left it to our enemies to construct our public image for us.

The literary theorist Gregory Jay has put the point well:

academic critics should not respond to their recent shellacking in the press by self-righteously bashing the media. Killing the messenger won't help, even when the message is inaccurate. While we have been busy in the last two decades producing a body of criticism and scholarly knowledge of extraordinary value, we have spent little time thinking about how to bring this work to bear on our society and our culture as a whole. If we feel misunderstood, part of the blame has to be our own. If we feel misrepresented, then we had better get to work representing ourselves and our work in more accessible and persuasive ways. This does not mean we have to sacrifice the institutionalized practices of highly specialized discourse . . . for a small audience. But it does mean that more of us should complement this kind of work with essays and books that translate our fields for the public and which argue for specific changes in our culture and our politics that follow from the research we have done. . . . This will give the reporters something easier to report accurately, though it will also mean exposing ourselves to the risk of public scrutiny and intense debate.[3]

What Jay recognizes here, I think, is that for all its ugliness and threat, the culture war now offers academic humanists an opportunity for the sort of entry into the public sphere that we have been unable or unwilling to manage on our own. Seizing this opportunity requires more, however, than simply *translating* oppositional theories and practices into language the public can understand. For these theories and practices could not be made accessible without undergoing a significant transformation, one that would mean respecting the objections of lay people instead of treating them as irredeemably naive or mystified.

I can imagine three possible outcomes to the culture war, which I want to set forth schematically here (with apologies for the somewhat cartoon-like opposition of left and right):

1. In outcome 1, the academic left is decisively defeated. Untenured radicals lose their jobs or are denied them, while established ones are so marginalized that they lose whatever power and influence they have achieved. Programs in women's and ethnic studies are shut down, and the expansion and diversification of the canon is arrested or reversed. In the name of halting "the McCarthyism of the Left," affirmative action is discontinued, while grants are denied to scholars judged to have a "political agenda."

This seems to me unlikely as a *general* outcome, though something like it seems already to be happening at the National Endowment for the Humanities, and if powerful figures like NEH's Lynne Cheney and Yale's Dean Kagan get their way, it could become the dominant national trend.

2. Whereas outcome 1 is frightening (to me, anyway), outcome 2 is merely dismal, but given our institutional history it seems more probable. In this outcome, we get nothing so dramatic as a general purge of the academic left. Rather, it becomes clear that neither side can win a decisive victory; eventually, the combatants becomes so exhausted or bored by the battle that they lose interest, and the controversy more or less collapses under the weight of its own acrimony. In this outcome, the culture war is "resolved" so to speak by an armed truce in which each side grudgingly agrees to accord the other its portion of the curricular and departmental turf on the tacit agreement not to interfere with one another. Radicals are licensed to go on problematizing as they please in their courses while traditionalists go on humanizing away in theirs. Professor Trendy dismantles the ideology of Western culture in one course, while Professor Redneck shores up the fragments of that culture in the same classroom the next hour. Their students assiduously write down the words of both, which count for the same number of credit-hours in the catalog.

This outcome would leave us, in effect, with two separate canons and two separate curricula that rarely communicate with one another. It is the state of affairs we may be in the process of evolving now.

3. Outcome 3 is the one that for me would be the most desirable, the "Thanks, we needed that" outcome. Professor Redneck and company not only fail to liquidate or disempower Professor Trendy, but in the process of trying are exposed in the eyes the public for their intolerance and anti-intellectualism. But instead of gloating over the embarrassment of the enemy, Professor Trendy and company learn a lesson about public representation. Not just the academic left, but the humanities and the academy generally emerge from the culture war with a chastened sense of the need to clarify and justify their enterprise to a wider public.

There are those, of course, who will object that any such clarification and justification would only provoke a yawn or a laugh. The suspicion is that were academic humanists ever so unwise as to become clearer in their work, they would only remove any remaining doubt that such work is so narrow and specialized that it *has* no potentially wider public. But the skeptics cannot have things both ways: an institution cannot be both inconsequential *and* dangerous at the same time. The academic humanities would hardly be getting into the news with such frequency if their concerns were still as pedantically circumscribed as they once were.

I am suggesting that today's humanistic research can make a better case for its educational and public potential than could the humanistic research of fifty years ago. For contrary to popular belief, this research is no longer the overspecialized thing it was when the English Institute held its first meeting in 1939. On the contrary, if the academic humanities are *over*-anything, they are *over*-generalized rather than overspecialized. For a generation now, the humanities have actually penalized narrow specialization and reserved their highest rewards for work that propounds sweeping cultural theories and broad interdisciplinary generalizations, work that promises to revise the paradigm for thinking about its subject.[4]

To see what I mean, one need only compare some of the typical paper-titles from the first English Institute program in 1939 and those in 1991: compare for example the papers in 1939 on such subjects as "Inflection as a Criterion of Dialect," "Lines of Demarcation in American Dialects," and "Editorial Revisions of Letters" with such topics on this year's program as "Multiculturalism and Criticism" and "Literature and Deterrence" (as well as the many papers over the past decade on such issues as the culture war, feminism, and gay studies). Then, too, to take another kind of evidence, consider the terms in which academic books are today promoted. We do not hear Oxford University Press boasting that its current list in criticism is more highly specialized than that of Harvard University Press. On the contrary, the claim is inevitably that one's list is path-breaking and frontier-crossing. That such claims usually have more to do with hype than sober accuracy should not obscure the fact that a shift in priorities has taken place, a path-breaking shift, one could say.

On the other hand, it is undeniable that our new theories and methods certainly *look* specialized and obscure: "Literature and Deterrence" will sound as mysterious to most lay people as "Inflection as a Criterion of Dialect," perhaps more mysterious since more unexpected. There is nevertheless a significant difference: if a discussion of literature and deterrence seems unclear to non-academics, it will probably be because of the specialized language in which it is couched, not because the subject has no potential general interest. The conclusion this suggests is that the humanistic academy has made itself look more specialized and obscure to lay people than it is or needs to be.

If this claim seems improbable in the face of today's journalistic attacks, I would argue that this very antagonism is a sign of increased closeness between the academic and the journalistic worlds. A generation ago, few journalists would have thought the preoccupations of academic humanists even worthy of hostile attention. That editorial pages are suddenly bristling with abuse of literature professors testifies to the extent to which the internal battles of the academy have become one with the battles being fought outside. It points up the fact that the academic humanities since World War II have ceased to be a purely antiquarian enterprise lending social veneer to their graduates and have begun to compete with the popular media as an alternative interpretation of American experience.

The very assault on "political correctness" paradoxically bespeaks a new closeness between the humanistic academy and the surrounding culture. Consider how often attacks on "PC" conflate the issue of ethnic slurs in student dormitories and the issue of multiculturalist revisions of the curriculum. Suspect as such a conflation may be—to favor the broadening of the curriculum is not necessarily to favor codes regulating so-called hate speech—it points up a connection that most educational progressives would themselves acknowledge between multiculturalism in curricular reform and sensitivity in personal relations. It is no accident that current debates over the validity of postcolonial interpretations of *The Tempest* overlap with debates over hiring and admissions, which in turn overlap with debates over affirmative action or the rights and status of minorities in the culture at large. Those who supported and those who opposed the appointment of neoconservative Carol Iannone to the NEH advisory council care about the same things.

In short, the very hostility that has been unleashed in the culture war is a sign of the shrinking distance between the academic humanities and the non-academic public. Such a situation creates a promising opportunity, though admittedly it is hard to be optimistic when you and your colleagues are regularly defamed in the press without being offered the courtesy of a reply. Even gross misrepresentations, however, can enable truths to leak out that were not generally visible before. The risk in broadcasting accusations of crimes against the humanities is that an opportunity will be created for the accused parties to tell their side of the story to an audience that otherwise would not hear it or even know it existed. A public scene may be created that did not exist before in which the orthodox representations can be contested. There is something to the show business maxim that bad publicity is better than no publicity at all—at least it *can* be better if it presents an opportunity to reshape and transform the terms of that publicity.

Obviously, this is a large and risky *if*. But there is far more risk in assuming there is nothing that can be done except to sit tight and hope that the present firestorm will blow over. The terms in which the humanistic academy is being publicly misrepresented will not be changed if academic humanists do not fight to change them.

This will not be easy, for reasons I have suggested. Overlaid on our old-fashioned distrust of popularization is a new-fangled distrust of popularization that stems from the fear of being co-opted—though this is a danger that seems less and less necessary to worry about. Having assiduously trained itself to speak in voices that could not be understood, much less appropriated by the likes of William Bennett, Allan Bloom, and Lynne Cheney, the academic left wakes up one day and finds itself without an idiom in which to challenge the misrepresentations being made of it by just these people. Though academic articles and books now teem with cogent critiques *of* the Bennetts, Blooms, and Cheneys, these critiques are rarely addressed *to* these figures themselves or to those inside and outside the academy who agree with their perception of things. Though these critiques create a useful solidarity among academic progressives, they are rarely addressed to anyone who is not already persuaded.

If little of the controversial new work in the humanities is amenable to journalistic popularization, I suspect this has less to do with its jargon or obscurity than with what it takes for granted as going without saying. This is not to agree with the nostalgic argument of critics like Russell Jacoby, who writes as if all would be well if progressive academics would drop their jargon and begin emulating Lionel Trilling (who, it seems to have been forgotten, was seen by many in his time as an often infuriatingly opaque writer). It is not their jargon that makes politically vanguard academics unpublishable in *Newsweek* so much as their tendency to assume an addressee who already takes their assumptions for granted, or at least does not need to have them spelled out. The habit of preaching to the converted seems to me a greater obstacle to the entry of academic progressive discourse into the public sphere than the more publicized problems of jargon and obscurity, though jargon and obscurity are themselves often a byproduct of preaching to the converted. What turns away lay audiences, I think, is the failure to take their assumptions into account except as instances of a naive or mystified consciousness that has to be unmasked.

Not that those on the right and center do not preach to the converted as much or more than the leftist dissenting academy does—and with vastly more power and effect, since preaching to the converted in the pages of *Newsweek* has immeasurably greater impact than doing so in the pages of *Cultural Critique.* But by its own argument, the academic left has less luxury to preach to the converted than do its conservative and centrist critics, since it has fewer converts. Preaching to the converted makes sense only if you assume you are winning.

It is ceasing to be enough to demonstrate again and again that what passes in our culture for apolitical common sense is often hegemonic ideology, even if this is often perfectly true. The proposition that "everything is political," by now such a commonplace in advanced academic discourse that it often goes without saying, remains a strange and counter-intuitive idea to most people outside the academy. Not only do those who most need to understand this proposition not agree with it, they do not have a clear notion what it means when they read it or see it referred to in the writings of academic radicals. If part of the reason is that there is a dominant ideology that makes it sound counter-intuitive to say that everything is political, it is also that those who make the argument rarely explain what it means, certainly not in a way that respects the resistances of those who do not already accept it. If those people's minds are to be changed, they need to have such formulations explained to them not just in language free of jargon, but in a tone that respects their skepticism and takes their counter-arguments seriously. That their skepticism may be ideologically motivated is all the more reason why it needs to be respected if it is to be overcome.

Terry Eagleton has recently made the point that "in the critique of ideology, only those interventions will work which make sense to the mystified subject itself."[5] Yet in the impressive flourishing of ideological critique in the academy over the last three decades, how much of this work even attempts to make sense to "the mystified subject"? To be sure, it is only recently that the presumably mystified subject has begun paying much attention, and perhaps has been inspired to do so only by a journalistic campaign of vilification. Again, however, this seems all the more reason why ideological critics need to start speaking in a rhetoric that addresses not only sympathetic academics, but those who figure to quarrel with their key assumptions and arguments.

A more public rhetoric is especially needed in today's curricular reform debates, where the political issues are increasingly being fought out. Yet I see little sign of such rhetoric in the growing body of writing calling for an oppositional curriculum, a transformative educational practice, a pedagogy of the oppressed. Current radical educational theory seems commonly to address a teacher who is *already* committed to social transformation and only lacks the lesson-plan for translating the commitment into classroom practice. Radical theorists never ask what role will be played in a radical curriculum by teachers and students who do not particularly wish to be radical. The assumption seems to be that radical pedagogy is for those who have already been radicalized (or have decided they wish to be), since the rest will presumably prefer to mind their own business. The current backlash suggests they do not intend to do that.

To see what I am talking about, consider the following statements from an essay by Henry Giroux, a leading advocate of educational reform:

The notion of the liberal arts [Giroux writes] has to be reconstituted around a knowledge-power relationship in which the question of the curriculum is seen as a form of cultural and political production grounded in a radical conception of citizenship and public wisdom.[6]

Giroux writes that students need to take up

a language of critique and possibility, a language that cultivates a capacity for reasoned criticism, for undoing the misuses of power and the relations of domination, and for exploring and extending the utopian dimensions of human potentiality.[7]

Such writing claims to be democratic yet it implicitly shuts out any reader, whether teacher, student, or non-academic, who does not already agree with its political premise. It shuts out the reader, for example, who might need to be persuaded that American cultural life is chiefly characterized by "misuses of power" and "relations of domination." In other words, it shuts out probably the vast majority of American students, parents, and educators.

So also does the claim by Giroux that follows from this assumption about American cultural life, that the liberal arts should be "reconstituted around a knowledge-power relationship" and the curriculum grounded in "a radical conception of citizenship." Such statements simply fail to speak to the numerous constituencies outside the leftist circle who would have to be centrally involved in any democratic transformation of the curriculum along the lines being proposed.

One can see a similar tendency to assume an already converted addressee in the current movement to establish cultural studies in the university. In fact, it seems fair to say that "cultural studies" has become a euphemism for leftist studies. I have argued in the past on behalf of cultural studies as the most promising available umbrella-concept for connecting and integrating the disciplines, and I do not intend to reverse myself.[8] But if the idea of cultural studies has no place for conservative, liberal, and other definitions of "culture" besides radical ones, it is likely to become yet another recipe for the self-marginalization of the left.

This is my one reservation about Patrick Brantlinger's excellent recent book, *Crusoe's Footprints: Cultural Studies in Britain and America*. On the one hand, Brantlinger properly sees cultural studies as a way to institutionalize "democratic values." On the other hand, his conception of cultural studies seems restricted to a by now familiar rainbow coalition of Marxists, "feminists, Afro-American and Ethnic Studies scholars, Foucauldians, deconstructive and hermeneutic 'radicals,' discourse theorists, and 'critical' social scientists . . . ."[9] Clearly, no members of the National Association of Scholars need apply. The founding gesture of cultural studies turns out to be the exclusion of anyone likely to say something about culture that might make academic leftists uncomfortable. In theory, cultural studies represents the acceptance of ideological and cultural difference, but in practice that difference is restricted to those who use "culture" in Raymond Williams's sense but not Matthew Arnold's.

I believe it is not in the long-range interest of the rainbow coalition to exclude its critics from its conception of cultural studies. A really democratic conception of cultural studies should be willing to risk opening itself to the considerable portion of humanity that would ask the kind of unfriendly questions that are not asked within the cultural left's cozy confines. This would include "naive" questions like, "Why characterize our culture in terms of 'relations of domination' when it is arguably more egalitarian than most other cultures?" and "Why is 'the language of critique' more important than the language of preserving tradition?" and "What does it mean to say that personal experience (or literature) is unavoidably political and ideological?" Cultural studies programs should be arenas for staging the debates among conflicting political interpretations of culture that the isolationism of academic departments has so often prevented from taking place.

The objection against this argument from the left tends to be that in a struggle for power, the left has to operate on the same self-protective principle as other academic power-groups always have. Why should feminists, Marxists, gay studies scholars, etc., invite conservatives onto the small portion of turf that they have carved out when those conservatives control so much of the university already, to say nothing of the culture itself? Though there are moments when such an argument may be expedient, it is worth reassessing its long-range adequacy, not only on educational grounds—the evasion of conflict being as deadening to the intellectual climate when practiced by the left as by the right—but on tactical grounds as well. One could, after all, think of an engagement with conservatives as a matter not of forfeiting turf that has been won by the left, but of entering and contesting the public sphere that is still dominated by those conservatives. The last thing the academic left would seem to need is yet another ghetto in which it endlessly reconfirms its own premises and turns its back on outsiders.

I bring the discussion down to the arena of curriculum and teaching because I think the chances of the academic humanities representing themselves more successfully than they have done up to now will depend to a large extent on whether the institutional patterns of daily work can be changed. That is, whether humanists cease preaching to the converted and begin talking to those outside their ranks will depend not simply on changes in individual writing and speaking habits. My view, which I have developed elsewhere, is that academics as a group are unlikely to begin writing and speaking more clearly and publicly until we stop teaching in isolated classrooms, which protect us from having to pay attention to the objections that would be raised by our colleagues down the hall or across the quad. Only a new organization of teaching, in which we teach with colleagues who are not afraid to disagree with us, is likely to train us to speak to those outside our friendly orbits. Teaching in a closed classroom to a captive audience of undergraduates or graduate students is poor training for dealing with people who disagree with you. It certainly does not provide the same experience in confronting intellectual challenges as does, for example, giving a talk at a conference or symposium like the present one—conditions we could begin reproducing in our day-to-day teaching operations.[10]

I am suggesting that there is a connection between our notorious unintelligibility to non-academics and the fact that we usually teach in isolation from our colleagues. In other words, clarifying what we do to outsiders has to be a collective not an individual project. A student today can go from one literature teacher who assumes that "the Western humanistic tradition" is uncontroversially above criticism to another teacher who refers uncontroversially to that tradition as an instance of "hegemonic discourse." Since the hypothetical student never sees these two teachers in dialogue, he or she may fail to recognize that they are referring to the same thing, that is, that they are in disagreement. Such a student is likely to be confused about the nature of both teacher's positions, which make sense only in relation to one another. These two teachers need one another in order to clarify their viewpoints to that student, but also to themselves.

So we need to stop thinking of the problem of public communication as a matter of individual teaching and writing and to start applying to the problem the kind of systematic terms we elsewhere use to think about organized mass-communications. Once again, we see how limited we are as long as we resist recognizing that the academy is a form of popular culture, a stance that prevents us from learning something from the media about the organization of representations. The media, after all, did not achieve their enormous influence without carefully thought-out efforts at collective organization. If the academy is also in the representation business, it has to think just as systematically about the organization of its representations.

It will be a salutary thing, then, if the current attacks on the academic humanities force them to rethink the conditions of academic communication in the public sphere. If we humanists refuse to learn something from these attacks about the need to engage with those who disagree with us, our critics will continue to succeed in monopolizing the rhetoric of democracy and in casting us as nattering nabobs of negativism. I have made the point elsewhere, but it bears repeating: if we are unable or unwilling to speak for ourselves in public, it will be our worst enemies who will speak for us.

NOTES

1. Robert E. Spiller, "Introduction," *English Institute Annual*; 1939 (New York: Columbia University Press, 1940), p. 3.

2. Michael Bérubé, "Political Correctness and the Media's Big Lie," *Village Voice*, XXXVI, no. 25 (June 18, 1991), p. 32.

3. Gregory Jay, unpublished talk delivered at session on "Academic Criticism and the Public Media," Modern Language Association annual convention, December, 1991.

4. I have developed this argument at greater length in two articles: "The Scholar in Society," forthcoming in Joseph Gibaldi, ed., *Introduction to Scholarship in Modern Languages and Literatures* (New York: Modern Language Association of America, 1992); "Academic Writing and the Uses of Bad Publicity," *South Atlantic Quarterly* 91:1 (Winter, 1992): 5–17. A few passages here repeat points made in these essays.

5. Terry Eagleton, *Ideology: An Introduction* (London: Verso, 1991), p. xiv.

6. Henry Giroux, "Liberal Arts Education and the Struggle for Public Life: Dreaming about Democracy," *South Atlantic Quarterly*, 89, no. 1 (Winter, 1990): 116.

7. Giroux, "Liberal Arts Education," p. 121.

8. See *Professing Literature: An Institutional History* (Chicago: University of Chicago Press), pp. 256ff.

9. Patrick Brantlinger, *Crusoe's Footprints: Cultural Studies in Britain and America* (New York: Routledge, 1990), p. 23.

10. For suggestions on how conferences can be used to connect courses, see Graff, "Other Voices, Other Rooms: Organizing and Teaching the Humanities Conflict," *New Literary History*, 21, no. 4 (Autumn, 1990): 817–839.

10.

Socratic Raptures, Socratic Ruptures: Notes Toward Queer Performativity

EVE KOSOFSKY SEDGWICK

I.

She resembles a recurrent
Scene from my childhood.
A scene called Mother Has Fainted.
Mother's body
Was larger, now it no longer moved;
Breathed, somehow, as if it no longer breathed.
Her face no longer smiled at us
Or frowned at us. Did anything to us.
Her face was queerly flushed
Or else queerly pale; I am no longer certain.
That it was queer I am certain.
—Randall Jarrell, "Hope"

The most dramatic thing that happened to me this summer was when I passed out for television. The TV cameras from the local news shows were there because we were having a demonstration, organized by an Ad Hoc Coalition of Black Lesbians and Gays, with participation from ACT UP-Triangle, against the University of North Carolina's local PBS station, which was refusing to air Marlon Riggs's *Tongues Untied,* a stunning film on the genocidally underrepresented topic of black gay men in the U.S. It was a muggy southern summer afternoon, by the side of a highway in Research Triangle Park. I had thought I was feeling strong enough for what looked to be a sedate demonstration (no civil disobedience), in spite of several months of chemotherapy which had pretty much decimated my blood cells.

But I guess I'd forgotten or repressed how arduous a thing it is any time a group of people try to project voices and bodies into a space of public protest that has continually to be reinvented from scratch, even though (or because) the protest-*function* is so routinized and banalized by the state and media institutions that enable it. You know what local news shows look like, how natural it seems that there should be, now and then, those shots of grim, dispirited people waving signs and moving their mouths, I mean moving our mouths, I mean yelling.

Yet the routinization of that tableau doesn't mean a lack of danger to the people occupying it. Arriving, I flashed onto a very different scene from New England a few winters earlier, when Amherst College, so pliant and responsive in matters curricular, stony and ruthless in matters managerial, had set out to do some (successful) union-busting at the quaint Lord Jeffrey Amherst Inn. On a ravishing Dickinsonian winter afternoon the concerned faculty—maybe five of us—and students gathered on the town green, holding signs, to silently "witness" the civil disobedience of a dozen union employees who were going to block traffic in front of the Inn and get arrested. The police had a yellow schoolbus there, everything was ready, and a beautiful, thick, silent and silencing snow began to fall. It was one of the first demonstrations I'd been a part of that wasn't a mass demonstration, and my heart, in spite of me, almost burst with exaltation at the spare and indicative Americanness of the scene, like reading Thoreau but also like a movie, at the pageant-like and intimately scaled democratic space of the town commons, at the patience of the highly choreographed police, at what seemed the thrilling symbolic leverage, within a tightly articulated legal discourse and history, of the protesters' most austere speech acts—silence, immobility, refusal—; at, I suppose, the secularized religiosity of my own function of "witnessing" this scene, another silent but apparently dense performative that made standing still with my mouth shut feel like embodying the whole Bill of Rights. It was the snow, profuse, gratuitous, equalizing, theatrically transformative, that seemed most to guarantee the totality and symbolic evenness of this pure, signifying space. It was also, however, the contingency of the snow that, in the slow unfolding of the afternoon, projected heart-stoppingly onto the largest screen the ambiguities about the "symbolic" standing of the protesters' refusals. Would the traffic stop for these anomalous figures in the road? *Could* it? Did they always know whether it could? Were nerves fraying? As protesters got read their rights, handcuffed, bundled off into the icing schoolbus, questions of standing devolved into dangerous questions of footing—it doesn't take much state force, in the twist of a policeman's wrist, in the simple not-thereness or symmetrical refusal of a policeman's arm, to send a handcuffed person crashing to the slippery ground. And it seemed puzzlingly as if the concrete and very contingent dangers of the scene, interfering on the pure symbolic register of civil disobedience, at the same time somehow were of its essence and indeed actually constituted its symbolic and performative power.

That was New England, though, and this was North Carolina, a New South whose stringy and desultory spaces seemed already built to provide a checkerboard of tedium and violence. Also that was a labor dispute, whose issues were always within referring distance of the great white scouring abstraction Money; while this was a fight about blackness, queerness, and (implicitly) AIDS—properties of bodies, some of them our bodies, of bodies that it is important to say most people are very willing, and many people murderously eager, to see not exist. I got there late, hugged and kissed friends I hadn't seen in a few weeks, and Brian gave me his sign to carry. I can't remember—I hardly noticed—what was on it, even though when I was a kid I remember that most of the symbolic power of the picket lines I saw used to seem to inhere in the voluntary self-violation, the then almost inconceivable willed assumption of stigma, that seemed to me to be involved in anyone's consenting to go public as a written-upon body, an ambulatory placard—a figure I, as a child, could associate only with the disciplining of children.[1] I wonder now how I related that voluntary stigma to the nondiscretionary stigma of skin color—that is, of skin color other than white—considering how fully, when I was growing up in the fifties and early sixties, "protest" itself implied black civil rights protest. It was at some distance from that childhood terror of the written-upon body—though not at an infinite distance—that, already wearing the black "Silence = Death" tee-shirt chosen because I thought it would read more graphically from a distance than my white ACT UP-Triangle tee-shirt, I gratefully took Brian's placard and commenced wagging it around with energy and satisfaction, as if to animate it with the animation of my own body and make it speak—to the TV cameras, to people in the cars that were passing, to the little line of demonstrators across the road. The heat, the highway, the outdoors, seemed to blot up voices and gestures and the chants that we hurled out of our lungs, trying exhaustingly to create a seamless curtain of rage and demand: "We're here, we're queer, and we won't pledge this year"; or better, "Snap! Snap! Snap! What is this racist crap?" There was also a lot of ACT UP's favorite funny chant, which makes me very nervous, a call-and-response borrowed from a heckler at an earlier demonstration of ours: one side rousingly yells "Freedom of speech!" and the other side responds "Shut up!"—"Freedom of speech!" "Shut up!"

The space of the demonstration was riddled, not only with acoustical sink-holes, but with vast unbridgeable gaps of meaning. It was in these gaps, or from out of them, that the force of any public protest might materialize, but into which, as well, it constantly risked dissolving. I think of the way our space was created and de-created, continually, by the raking attentions and sullen withdrawals of, on the one hand, the state troopers— the pathetically young and overdressed white state troopers, who at the same time looked totally out of it in their sweltering uniforms and yet effortlessly, through the same uniforms and because they had guns and radios, commanded all the physical presence and symbolic density that we were struggling to accrue, who made a space of their own ostentatiously apart from the demonstrators, ostentatiously "neutral," untouchable by the force of anything we could shout; but who had also the function of radiating jags of menace in our direction, shards of volatile possibility that boomeranged around in the aether of our expression—and, on the other hand, from another direction, the TV cameras, actually a complex of trucks, tripods, portable and stationary machines, and white people to occupy both ends of them: camera people, insolent with implicit dare and promise, to take them for walks along the line of our faces and bodies; and pretty girl and boy reporters to make a foreground to which our angry bodies could serve as background, generating the depth of field, the assurance of perspective and ten-foot-pole distance, for which television news serves as guardian and guarantee.

The uses we had for this news apparatus, as opposed to the uses it had for us, I condensed in my mind under the double formulation "shaming and smuggling." With the force of our words—referentially, that is—our object was to discredit the hollow pretense at "representing" the public maintained by our local "public" broadcasting station; to shame them into compliance or negotiation on the issue of airing this rare and important film. With the force of our bodies, however—and in that sense performatively—our object was not merely to demand representation, representation elsewhere, but ourselves to give, to *be* representation: somehow to smuggle onto the prohibitive airwaves some version of the apparently unrepresentably dangerous and endangered conjunction, *queer* and *black*.

Our need to be exemplary bodies sprang from the history of radical denial of exemplary function to black gay bodies at the intersection of two kinds of community that seem so often to carve each other out of perceptual existence: a tacitly racist white gay community for whom a black queer body, however eroticized, might stand as a representation of blackness but could never seem to embody queerness itself; and a more or less openly homophobic African-American community by whom the queerness of any black figure must be denied, suppressed, or overridden in order for that figure to be allowed to function as an embodiment of black identity or struggle. The denial by white communities, including white gay ones, of the subjectivity, agency, and representational efficacy of African-American selves is evidenced by, among other things, the clamorous absence of black people among represented subjectivity positions in white gay popular culture. An example of the more complicated place of gay identity within African-American political culture is the 1991 controversy in which the California Librarians Black Caucus persuaded the Los Angeles City Librarian to withdraw a Lesbian and Gay History Month poster that quoted a poem by Langston Hughes. Joyce Sumbi, an officer in the black librarians' group, wrote that use of the Hughes quotation, and the concomitant implication of Hughes's homosexuality, "would be insensitive and divisive at a time when African-Americans have set unity as [a] major goal."[2] Seemingly, this avoidance of division is to be achieved by a radical representational scission of the sexual identity of a significant proportion of African-American people.

The ambitions of our group of demonstrators—shaming, smuggling—were distinct, but in order for either ambition to be effective, they had to be presented together as one. The assertion that black queer absence gave the lie to the claims of a representatively "public" use of the airwaves could take its point only from the patent availability, indeed the assertive presence of such bodies. The protest function also, however, offered pretext and legitimacy to the presence of such bodies: it seems likely that our protest was the first occasion on which local TV in central North Carolina was constrained to offer images of people explicitly self-classified under the rubrics of black queer identity.

Shaming, smuggling: the two ambitions gesture at, and in a sense can stand for, a tradition of philosophical/linguistic play between constative utterances and performative ones. Shaming, constatively: "The inclusive representation you, North Carolina Public Television, have claimed to offer of this society demonstrably excludes a constituent part of it"—a verifiable, referential assertion about something away over there. Smuggling, performatively: "Present! *Ecce homo*"—a self-validating, hence self-referential form of meaning guaranteed by its relation to embodiment.

And yet I can't claim for the twinned ambitions behind this demonstration the supposedly clean distinctions between constative and performative, or between reference and embodiment. Few words, after all, could be more performative in the Austinian sense than "shame": "Shame on you," "For shame," or just "Shame!," the locutions that give sense to the word, do not describe or refer to shame, but themselves confer it. At the same time, our "smuggling" activity of embodiment, however self-referential, could boast of no autonomy from the circuits of representation. *At least* because a majority of our smuggling-intent bodies were not themselves black, many of us who had so much the need to make a new space for black queer representation were haplessly embroiled in the processes of reference—reference to other bodies standing beside our own, to the words on our placards, to what we could only hope would be the sufficiently substantial sense—if, indeed, even *we* understood it rightly—of our own intent.

After awhile I could tell I was feeling tired and dizzy; sensibly, I sat down. There was something so absorbing and so radically heterogeneous about this space of protest that when, next thing I knew, the urgent sound of my name and a slowly dawning sense of disorientation suggested that I seemed very oddly to be stretched out in the dirt—coming to—surfacing violently from the deep pit of another world—with a state trooper taking my pulse and an ambulance already on the way—the gaping, unbridgeable hole left in my own consciousness felt like a *mise-en-abîme* image of the whole afternoon; not least because the image, a compelling one on which both TV cameras were converging, hindered by protestors who struggled to block their sightlines ("Now *that's* censorship," the TV people rumbled, with some justice)—that image, of a mountainous figure, supine, black-clad, paper-white, weirdly bald (since my nice African hat had pitched to a distance), SILENCE = DEATH emblazoned, motionless, apparently female, uncannily gravid with meaning, but with what possible meaning? what usable meaning?, was available to everybody there except herself.

2.

As people arrive, no music, only silence. I like such awkward silences, though many resist them, especially in my classes. But a lot goes on during them.
— Michael Lynch, instructions for his memorial service, February 1990

The meaning with which that body was so dense, too dense, was indeed not a usable one (call me the face on the cutting-room floor) in relation to the complexly choreographed performative agendas and effects of that demonstration. But what has it got to do with the Places of Literary Criticism, or specifically with the issues of pedagogy to which my rapturous/rupturous title seems to promise to refer? The obvious connection for me is that most of the bodies and voices of friends at either side of me during the *Tongues Untied* protest, most of the alarmed faces of friends crowded over me when I came to, the voices in which I heard my own name, the backs and hands that blocked cameras, the hands that designed the signs and the voices that planned and rounded up people for the demonstration in the first place—so many of those voices, bodies, faces are the ones I also encounter in the seminar room. The people I teach gay and lesbian studies to are also the people whom, when I can do it, I do gay and lesbian activism with. I don't think such an arrangement is atypical of people doing politicized scholarship currently; for queer scholars lucky enough to be working with graduate students in the area, it certainly makes an important feature of the Way We Live Now. And if this suggests a utopian continuity between the space of the classroom and that of "the real world," it would be truer to say that it renders all the more inescapable, within the classroom and within the texts that activate us there, the discontinuities and decenterings that make the reality of "the real world." I like to brood over the reconstruction of that moment when I fainted partly because, through my absentation, it seems to place me however briefly at the center of the work of protest—as though I were Alice Walker's luminous vacuum of a heroine Meridian, say, whose narcoleptic presence/absence seems the perfect condensation of her contagious unconsciousness of fear, her uncanny talent for crystallizing loss and rage as socially embodied defiance and movement.

I wish I had those meridional traits, but can only wish it; if that sprawling body offered testimony, it was less to a triumphal purposefulness than to a certain magnetic queerness (by magnetic I mean productive of deviance) in the process called "demonstration." What felt to me like an almost telescopic condensation of the protest event embodied, as the most radical condensations will, less the power of condensation than of the displacements of meaning that interline it. (Displacements: The white skin of someone to whom black queer invisibility had come to feel—partly through representational work like *Tongues Untied,* partly in the brutalities of every day's paper, partly through transferentially charged interactions with students— like an aching gap in the real; the legible bodily stigmata not of AIDS but of a "female" cancer whose lessons for living assertively and powerfully with I find myself learning largely from men with AIDS; the defamiliarization and indeed the gaps of derecognition toward my "own" "female" "white" body, experienced under the pressure of amputation and prosthesis, of drugs, of the more than gender-destabilizing—I would say the gender-explosive—event of female baldness; the way in which, whatever one's privilege, a person living with a grave disease in this particular culture is inducted ever more consciously, ever more needily, yet with ever more profound and transformative revulsion into the manglingly differential world of health care under American capitalism.) It is with joy, with chagrin, with intense discomfort, that I have come to feel such displacements more and more in the condensing and complexly representative space of the classroom, as well—a classroom space regularly reconstituted by threat and mourning, and by the bareness of the cognitive and performative resistances we are able to mount to them. Finding myself as teacher, as exemplar, as persuader, as reader to be less and less at the center of my own classroom, I also find that the voice of a certain abyssal displacement—and mine is certainly not the only such displacement going on in these classrooms—can provide effects that may sometimes wrench the boundaries of discourse around in productive if not always obvious ways.

I feel as though the best pedagogical ideas (and there aren't many of them) that I've had about how to get stronger and stranger leverage on such processes have had to do with bringing more to life the bafflingly complex kind of *representational* space that a classroom is. Condensing and displacing the conditions of the surrounding world, always anachronistic (in more ways than one) in relation to it,[3] chronically the object of conflicting claims, needs, and strictures regarding its representational status, the college classroom also represents or misrepresents *differently* each of the different dimensions of experience and identity that constitute its inhabitants. For many of us, especially those coming out of traditions of feminist or liberation pedagogy, a strong motivating ambition in relation to the classroom is the utopian. One experiment that has been very important to me has been to try to reconstitute as many of my classes as possible as spaces in which the presumption about people's sexuality, the default position, will be, not the heterosexist libel-law presumption of the surrounding world that everyone is straight unless proven or "self-confessed" otherwise, but rather that everyone is probably queer until they individually make the decision—which many, I'm glad to say, avail themselves of the privilege of foregoing—to go public as straight. In some classes I've gone so far as to include in the syllabus a request that students who consider themselves heterosexual find ways of *not* making that information available to the rest of the class until, say, three weeks into the semester: until, that is to say, ideally, a time when they have been able to register the presumption of their queer-ness, not as an outlandish if educative burden, but rather precisely as—in relation to this particular cognitive and erotic space, and who knows, maybe even in relation to others—something to be explored, expanded, and prized.

I have also been finding it increasingly difficult to teach any kind of literature or theory, at least at the graduate level, without trying to involve students very actively in what might be called the experimental aspects of critical writing. Asking or encouraging students at this anxiously liminal, pre-professional stage to be numb to the performative force of their own writing strikes me as mutilating both to them and to the profession. A first assignment I often use is to talk briefly about Austin's description of performative utterances and then, very simply, to ask each student to bring to the next class a performative which they will actually do: something, that is, that will have been effectively done by the end of the class that wouldn't have been done otherwise: an invitation (but this means it has to be to a real party), a dare, a contract, a dedication. To some graduate students it is startling to be reminded that written words, their own, actually do things other than be evaluated. Beyond that, there is so much to be learned not only from the difficulty of doing the assignment, but from the many ways it's hard to tell whether or not, in a particular case, it has been effectually done; and, especially, from exploring the identities, the posi-tionalities, the temporalities, the particular communities, the enforcing agencies, the entire presumptive worlds that spring up in the interpellatory relations that surround and enable each performative utterance.

Another assignment that I and some students have learned a lot from begins with reading two essays—the ones I used were Leo Bersani's "Is the Rectum a Grave?" and Jan Brown's "Sex, Lies, and Penetration: A Butch 'Fesses Up"[4]—that are both structured around pivotal moments of saying, in Bersani's words, "In short, to put the matter polemically and even rather brutally, we have been telling a few lies."[5] Asking students to write a paper structured around "in short, we have been telling a few lies" turned out to be a good means of access to the powerful, contradictory ways in which the hermeneutics of disillusion and demystification, so intimately at the heart of the most influential writing projects and the most compelling truth-effects in this intellectual world, also construct highly stylized and conflicting reading positionalities in relation to the author and to authority, to identity politics, and to various imagined and enforced communities of address.

Another exercise that I know could be important, but haven't yet found a usable format for, would explore the complex relations of performativity and address that surround mourning, memorializing, and obituary functions, especially in politicized contexts. The closest I've gotten to this so far was in the very worst class hour I spent last semester—it was during the week when I was waiting for the breast cancer diagnosis, and when a good friend of my co-teacher's and mine and of several of our students seemed to be near death from AIDS in a distant city—when I had the bright idea that the way to approach teaching Freud's "Group Psychology and the Analysis of the Ego" would be to bring into class and read aloud the bitter, abusive, scatalogically paranoid, and to some degree irrefutable obituary address delivered by Larry Kramer, an AIDS activist, at the memorial service for the film critic Vito Russo after his death from AIDS last fall.[6] I don't think I was the only person in the class whom the performance of this text not only made break down, but rendered sullenly non-functional: so close did it come to the raw of the aggressions, guilts, identificatory adhesions, and foundational wounds and losses that made the possibility, and often the terrible painfulness, of *our* little primal horde.

3.

                        the interval
            Experience between
            And most profound experiment
            Appointed unto Men—
                    —Emily Dickinson (822)

I think what I am trying to bring together in saying all this are two traditions of meaning for the verb "perform"—meanings that I would suggest intersect, if they do at all, at a very odd angle somewhere in a neighborhood called queer. I am following up here on Judith Butler's invitation to "consider gender, for instance, as *a corporeal style,* an 'act,' as it were, which is both intentional and performative, where 'performative' itself carries the

double-meaning of 'dramatic' and 'non-referential.' "[7] Both demonstrating
and teaching—for that matter, of course, lecturing—obviously enough constitute performance in the quasi-theatrical, "extroverted" sense of corporeal/
linguistic acts structured by the presumption of a spectatorial consumer in
the offing. However, no doubt more can be said of performative *speech-
acts* than that they are introversively "non-referential," in the context of
an activism where bodies continually struggle to constitute themselves as
transformative forms of utterance at an interface with the most routinizing
machineries of representation; or in the context of pedagogy where issues
of exemplariness come into such an unstable relation with the more explicit
issues of cognition and of persuasion. Following on de Man's demonstration
of "a radical estrangement between the meaning and the performance of
any text,"[8] one might, in the context of figures that so urgently intend
meaning, want to ponder not so much the non-reference of the performative
but rather (what de Man calls) its necessarily "aberrant"[9] relation to its
own reference—its queer referentiality, we might want to say.

If I seem to be using "queer" in a slippery way in this formulation,
hovering uneasily between meaning "unaccountable" and meaning "homosexual," that is quite to the point of various scandals that make a difference
in the history of the relation between performing something and saying it:
foundationally, the inextricable and unrationalizable origin, with Plato, of
the language of philosophical speculation *tout court* in a series of scripted
pedagogical dramas of pederastic seduction/refusal; more historically, what
I have been arguing for several years now is the installation, at the beginning
of the present century, of two very specific and philosophically anomalous
kinds of speech acts, "closetedness" and "coming out," in the most centrally
indicative relation to notions of truth and self (which is among other things
to say, following Foucault, to notions of sexuality) across our present cultures. Foucault's "demonstrations" themselves constitute founding instances
of queer performativity. Given Foucault's immensely productive and I
believe still radically underexplored critique of the repressive hypothesis,
for example, as I have written elsewhere, no doubt it will be clear why his
History of Sexuality was to prove so catalytic for literary study:

Coarsely put: it justifies a view of writing as a form of sex, indeed as its
most direct form; at the same time it justifies a view of sexuality as the
central repository of the truth-values of modernity. How could these not
be deeply energizing assertions for writers and scholars—at least if Foucault
is right in his estimate of the prestige, the promise of epistemological force,
the "sex appeal," of sexuality in our century? This is also to say, of course,
that, far from offering resistance to the modern "scheme for transforming
sex into discourse" (20) and "interplay of truth and sex" (57), processes
that Foucault treats as historically unidirectional and inescapable, the effect

of his book has instead been to accelerate that trajectory and load it with
ever greater explanatory force. Rather than attempt vainly to impede it,
he has, if successful, merely *displaced* and re-propelled it unpredictably by
making less tenable the "repressive hypothesis" by which its subjects have
concealed its itineraries from themselves. "Merely" displaced and re-propelled: but that is a more direct path of rhetorical efficacy—of historical
intervention, which is to say, in Foucault, of seduction—than most critical
works admit to undertaking. Thus, again excitingly for any writer, this
work has seemed to offer new accesses to the performative force of writing.
In the unmentioned, only slightly displaced continuity between what the
book *says* and what it seems to *make happen,* readers can register the gap
of unrationalized rhetorical force that the author has already thematized in
the distance between what the "repressive hypothesis" says (sex is forbidden) and the almost hilarious proliferation of sexualized discourse that it
in fact effects.[10]

I would also mention, though I don't have the space here to do justice to
its intricacies, the way in which the rhetorical force and the complex reader
relations of Foucault's *History of Sexuality* can be shown repeatedly to
depend on precisely the reductive, identity-bound homo/hetero definitional
split that the book's more overt project is to deconstruct—with the results,
among others, that homosexuality is effectually installed there in a more
than just metonymic relation to sexuality as a whole, which is to say to
identity and truth; and that the disposal of homo/heterosexual identifications in and around the book repeatedly (and, I would add, appropriately)
positions the closet and coming out as the central, silent, indexical referents
for confession and for the repressive hypothesis.
  It concerns me that the force of Foucault's critique of the repressive
hypothesis has been radically neutralized, in much subsequent engagé criticism conducted more or less in his name, by numb refusals to register the
pressure of and, as it were, to participate however resistantly in what can
never be more or less than the oblique and queer performance of that
critique. In a myriad of ways in contemporary thought—ways in which
Foucault himself was hardly unimplicated—his critique of the repression
hypothesis has been all but fully recuperated in new alibis *for* the repression
hypothesis: in neatly symmetrical celebrations of "productive" "multiplic-
ities" of "resistance" (to what if not to repression); in more glamorously
pessimistic mappings of the performative ruses and ubiquitous double binds
of carceral repression, mappings that seem not to have motivated readers
to account to themselves for the strictly segregated, paroxystically aesthetic
pleasures that at the same time motivate and underpin them;[11] finally in
all the dreary and routine forms of good dog/bad dog criticism by which,
like good late-capitalist consumers, we persuade ourselves that deciding

what we like or don't like about what's happening is the same thing as actually intervening in its production.

The critical practice most responsive to these concerns and possibilities would be, I think, something more properly described as *experimental* critical writing than as what has come to be called "personal criticism," valuable as the latter project has been. The space between "experiential" and "experimental" is admittedly small—from ancient Greek to nineteenth-century English, the denotation of first-person undergoing and that of deliberate evidential trial have remained compacted in the same syllables. And it's suggestive that the scientism of one meaning—experiment—and the subjectiveness of the other—experience—should be tethered so closely together. As a queer activist writer, am I more like the genetic engineer or the guinea pig? To make such a question less ugly and reductive requires destabilization and diffusion of the "I" in it: operations that a genuinely experimental criticism can hardly help but effect. An attention to the framework of experimental staging is also necessary: in criticism as in science, in science as in criticism, it is always worth asking what onlookers are interpellated, and how, in the establishing theatrics of experimental authority.

That the effects of such experiments are radically unpredictable is, obviously, to the point of their queer performativity; "that they are queer I am certain," as Randall Jarrell would put it; but how, by whom, and in what relations "queerness" itself may be constituted is still up for grabs both within and outside of the academy. Part of the specificity of its positioning between "inside" and "outside" is that unlike the anti-racist, anti-sexist, secularist, and anti-ablest components that are also currently being ascribed to "politically correct" ideology, this one not only isn't the law of the land but in most cases, in most places, must go directly against it. Legally, for example, the Constitution enshrines the rights of secularity, and has been effectually interpreted as conferring equal protection on the basis of gender and abledness as well as race—but not, as we know, of sexual orientation. The military, most churches, the CIA, and public education, to mention only a few plausible professions, are still unblinking about wanting to exclude suspected lesbians and gay men, while in only a tiny handful of places in the U.S. does anyone have even nominal legal protection against the routine denial of employment, housing, insurance, custody, or other vital rights on the basis of her or his perceived or supposed sexual orientation. Even institutions that want to extend equal protections to lesbians and gay men can be legally prevented from doing so: in the twenty-five states that have anti-sodomy laws, for example, *Bowers v. Hardwick* is now regularly misapplied in this way. Thus if a lot of colleges now include, as they do, sexual orientation as a category in their stated commitments to equal opportunity, that places them in a relation of high tension with their surroundings. The space of our curricular innovation, like the space of our writing and meditation, is hard-won and precarious. What the gay movement has had to depend on in place of any state support whatever is, quite simply, speech and visibility. That speech and visibility are complex acts—that they may necessarily be internally contradictory; that they may necessarily, as well, contradict each other in explosive and unpredictable ways—does not gainsay that it is only speech and visibility that legitimate us. It is speech and visibility that give us any political power we have. It is speech and visibility that apparently make us threatening. It is our new speech and assertive visibility that have fueled the resurgent epidemic of homophobic violence. The stunning impact of a group like ACT UP comes, not in the first place from the moral gravity of its program of civil disobedience, but rather from its skill at making the rage, loss, and even pleasure of a large group of people visible, audible, graphically apprehensible. Our speech and visibility have been incalculably powerful in the politics of the electorate, of the media, of the space of the streets— powerful *for* us; powerful when used *against* us; powerful in ways we can never expect fully to control; but to which, for a politicized body of queer, queer-loving, and anti-homophobic citizens, scholars, teachers, there is very starkly no alternative.

NOTES

1. There is more discussion of this figure in my essay, "A Poem is Being Written," *Representations* 17 (Winter, 1987): 745–757, especially pp. 125–6.

2. Scott Harris, "Battle Lines: Use of Hughes Poem on Gay History Poster Ignites Furor," *Los Angeles Times,* June 13, 1991, pp. B1, B4, quotation from p. B4.

3. I discuss this further in an essay, "Gender Criticism: What Isn't Gender," in Stephen Greenblatt and Giles Gunn, eds., *Redrawing the Boundaries of Literary Study in English* (New York: MLA, 1992), forthcoming. From that essay:

It is very hard to come up with useful images for the synecdochic relation of academic institutions to the larger world of productive institutions in our culture. One important thing about academia is how drastically it tends to *condense*. The very name of the *univer*sity conveys that its ambition is to represent something huge in a disproportionately tiny space—a space that thereby tends to be rendered, of course, unreal or hyperreal, so that the desublimation of its *un*transformed relations across the local "real"—for instance, its infrastructural labor relations, its health-care provisions, its effects on real estate values and municipal tax bases, its symbiosis with various industries and communities—requires repeated wrenching acts of re-recognition. Moreover, the condensation that the university effects on its universe is not only uneven but tendentious, partial, and intermittent in its coverage: increasingly important segments of the society can seem to escape its purview entirely.

Beyond being condensed, and thus tending toward the unreal or the hyperreal, in its synecdochic relation to the universe it claims to represent, the university is also in an anachronistic relation to it. People may choose an academic vocation, not in the first place because of their cognitive talents or because they have particular political values or identifications, but because academic labor, at least at its most privileged and visible levels, is still in many ways so amazingly unrationalized. Compared to industrial or to other service labor—even compared to the other professions—our fealty to the stop-clock and to time discipline, to the bottom line of profitable or even of quantifiable results, to the public/private stresses of office or factory interaction, to the suppression or denial of affective charge, and in particular to the forcible alienation of our labor in the service of projects conceived by and for someone else, is still, for some, almost miraculously attenuated. Projects conceived in relation to identity politics, such as feminist or gay/lesbian inquiry, are continually testing and redefining the limits of such a professional exemption. Delusive as some of these freedoms may be, the space of work for at least some in this industry can seem strikingly close to an idealized pre-industrial workspace of task orientation, work continuity, and the relatively meaningful choice of tasks based on perceptible need and aptitude.

The complex temporality of our representational space has a variety of consequences. First and most obviously, it means that academia and academics are always almost definitionally in danger of embodying various simply nostalgic or reactionary politics. Second, it means that the many, very distinctly rationalized and alienating aspects of academic labor, which form all or most of the conditions of work for so very many academics, always risk being occluded or mystified by this more elegiac ideal. Third, it of course marks the vulnerability of this space to the scouring triumphalism of capitalist rationalization; while the relatively decentered structure and diffuse status-economy of U.S. higher education pose some resistance to our instant, wholesale Thatcherization, this state's hypersensitivity to interventions into the discourses of gender and of homo/heterosexuality, in particular, may represent the threshold of an extreme risk. Fourth and more encouragingly, our anomalous temporality is one of the things that allows academia to function as a kind of cognitive gene-pool of precisely anachronistic ideas, impulses, or information that, un-usable under one set of political circumstances, might be preserved in this relatively unrationalized space to emerge with a potentially priceless relevance under changed ones. And fifth, I think many of us are very responsive to the utopian potential of this vision of a form of relatively unalienated, sometimes collaborative labor. No less dangerously grounded in the retrospect than any other utopian formation, it can nevertheless afford energies and leverages for change both within and around the institution.

4. Jan Brown, "Sex, Lies, and Penetration," *Out/Look* 7 (Winter, 1990): 30–34.

5. Leo Bersani, "Is the Rectum a Grave?," in Douglas Crimp, ed., *AIDS: Cultural Analysis, Cultural Activism* (Cambridge, Mass.: MIT Press, 1988), pp. 197–222, quoted from p. 206.

6. To quote:

We killed Vito. As sure as any virus killed him, we killed him. Everyone in this room killed him. 25 million people outside this room killed him. . . .

Vito was the most beloved gay man I know. I've ever known. And gay men killed him. And lesbians.

. . . . If Moses or Jesus or Joan of Arc came along to lead us, we'd shit all over them and throw them out.

. . . . There ain't no cures yet, boys and girls. There should have been by now. There would have been by now if we were all straight and white and male and middle-class. There would have been by now if 25 million gay men and lesbians had their act together. But we didn't. And they shit all over us. Day after day they shit huge turds all over us. And Vito's dead. And everyone in here knows plenty who are dead. We killed them. And I'm going to be dead. And 20 million HIV-infected by the year 2000 are going to be dead.

Larry Kramer, "Who Killed Vito Russo?," *Outweek*, February 20, 1991, p. 26.

7. Judith Butler, "Performative Acts and Gender Constitution: An Essay in Phenomenology and Feminist Theory," in Sue-Ellen Case, ed., *Performing Feminisms: Feminist Critical Theory and Theatre* (Baltimore and London: The Johns Hopkins University Press, 1990), pp. 270–282, quoted from pp. 272–273.

8. Paul de Man, *Allegories of Reading: Figural Language in Rousseau, Nietzsche, Rilke, and Proust* (New Haven and London: Yale University Press, 1979), p. 298.

9. ". . . far from closing off the tropological system, irony enforces the repetition of its aberration." *Allegories,* p. 301.

10. From "Gender Criticism: What Isn't Gender." See also Michel Foucault, *The History of Sexuality, Volume I: An Introduction,* trans. Robert Hurley (New York: Vintage Books, 1980).

11. Let me clarify that my problem isn't with this writerly project itself, in which a number of important New Historicist writers seem to participate, and of which the writing of a critic like D.A. Miller might be taken as exemplary; the strange angles at which the formal energy of this writing careens off from its paraphraseable argument offer, to the contrary, one of the most exciting models of resistant participation in "what can never be more or less than the oblique performance" of a critique of the repression hypothesis. Rather I have issue to take with the many dutiful readers who ignore its aestheticizing energies and repress how unexpected a spin these energies may impart to the arguments they propel.

Contributors

JOHN BRENKMAN teaches at Baruch College and the Graduate Center of the City University of New York. He is the author of *Culture and Domination* and *Theorizing Males: A Cultural Critique of the Oedipus Complex*.

LESLIE FIEDLER, SUNY Distinguished Professor and Samuel Clemens Professor of English at the State University of New York at Buffalo, is the author of more than 25 books, most recently *Fiedler on the Roof*. Famous for his provocative views and passionate devotion to a non-elitist look at popular culture, Fiedler has earned numerous awards and prizes for his criticism and fiction. He has lectured all over the world and many of his writings have been translated into other languages.

STANLEY FISH is Arts and Sciences Professor of English and Professor of Law at Duke University. His most recent book is *Doing What Comes Naturally: Change, Rhetoric, and the Practice of Theory in Literary and Legal Studies* (1989). The present essay is part of a collection of pieces on cultural conflict in and out of the university to be published within the year by Oxford University Press.

JANE GALLOP teaches in the Modern Studies Graduate Program at the University of Wisconsin. Her books include *Reading Lacan, The Daughter's Seduction, Intersections, Thinking Through the Body,* and *Around 1981: Academic Feminist Literary Theory*.

HENRY LOUIS GATES, JR. is W.E.B. Du Bois Professor of the Humanities at Harvard University. His books include *Figures in Black, The Signifying Monkey,* and *Loose Canons: Notes on the Culture Wars.*

JONATHAN GOLDBERG is Sir William Osler Professor of English Literature at The Johns Hopkins University. His most recent books include *Sodometries: Renaissance Texts, Modern Sexualities* and *Writing Matter: From the Hands of the English Renaissance.* He is co-editor, with Stephen Orgel, of the Oxford Authors *John Milton,* and editor of two forthcoming volumes, *Queering the Renaissance* and *The Sodomy Reader.*

GERALD GRAFF became George M. Pullman Professor of English and Education at the University of Chicago in 1992 after having taught since 1966 at Northwestern University. He is the author of *Professing Literature: An Institutional History* (Chicago, 1987), and his *Beyond the Cultural Wars: How Teaching the Conflicts Can Revitalize American Education* will be published by W.W. Norton in the fall of 1992.

SUSAN GUBAR is Distinguished Professor of English and Women's Studies at Indiana University. With Sandra M. Gilbert, she has written *The Madwoman in the Attic, The War of the Words, Sexchanges,* and edited the *Norton Anthology of Literature by Women.* They have just completed a satiric book, "Masterpiece Theatre: An Academic Melodrama," on the state of English studies at the present time.

GEOFFREY HARTMAN, Professor of English and Comparative Literature at Yale University, has published many books on literature and theory, including *Wordsworth's Poetry, Criticism in the Wilderness,* and most recently *Minor Prophecies: The Literary Essay in The Culture Wars.* He was a Trustee of the English Institute from 1976 to 1986.

JONATHAN Z. KAMHOLTZ is Associate Professor of English and Comparative Literature at the University of Cincinnati, where he also currently serves as Academic Director for Humanities and Social Sciences for the College of Evening and Continuing Education.

ALVIN KERNAN is Avalon University Professor of Humanities, Emeritus, Princeton University. He is presently Senior Advisor in the Humanities to the Andrew W. Mellon Foundation and the director of the Mellon Fellowships in Humanistic Studies. His most recent writing on this subject is *The Death of Literature* (Yale University Press, 1990).

EVE KOSOFSKY SEDGWICK is Newman Ivey White Professor of English at Duke University, and is the author of *Between Men: English Literature and Male Homosocial Desire* and *Epistemology of the Closet.*